T H E   B O O K   O F

Desserts

T H E   B O O K   O F

Desserts

SALLY TAYLOR

Photographed by
DAVID GILL

Published by Salamander Books Limited
LONDON • NEW YORK

Published 1990 by Salamander Books Ltd.,
129/137 York Way, London N7 9LG

This book was created by Merehurst Limited
Ferry House, 51-57 Lacy Road, Putney, London SW15 1PR

© 1990 Salamander Books Ltd.

ISBN: 0 86101 285 2

Commissioned and directed by Merehurst Limited
Managing Editor: Felicity Jackson
Designer: Sue Storey
Recipes by Sally Taylor and Caroline Cowen
Home Economists: Janice Murfitt (pages 10, 11, 12, 13, 14,
15, 18, 19, 22, 23, 26, 27, 30, 31, 34, 35, 36, 38, 44, 45, 46,
47, 52, 53, 54, 55, 58, 59, 62, 64, 66, 67, 70, 71, 76, 77, 80,
81, 84, 85, 88, 92, 93, 94, 95, 96, 98, 99, 101, 102, 103,
106, 110, 112, 113, 116 and 118)
Mandy Wagstaff (pages 8, 9, 16, 17, 20, 21, 24, 25, 28, 29,
32, 33, 37, 39, 40, 41, 42, 43, 48, 49, 50, 51, 56, 57, 60, 61,
63, 65, 68, 69, 72, 73, 74, 75, 78, 79, 82, 83, 86, 87, 89, 90,
91, 97, 100, 104, 105, 107, 108, 109, 111, 114, 115, 117
and 119)
Photographer: David Gill
Typeset by Angel Graphics
Colour separation by Scantrans Pte Ltd, Singapore
Printed in Belgium by Proost International Book
Production, Turnhout

Companion volumes of interest:
The Book of COCKTAILS
The Book of CHOCOLATES & PETITS FOURS
The Book of HORS D'OEUVRES
The Book of GARNISHES
The Book of PRESERVES
The Book of SAUCES
The Book of ICE CREAMS & SORBETS
The Book of GIFTS FROM THE PANTRY
The Book of PASTA
The Book of HOT & SPICY NIBBLES – DIPS – DISHES
The Book of CRÊPES & OMELETTES
The Book of FONDUES
The Book of BISCUITS
The Book of CHEESECAKES
The Book of PIZZAS & ITALIAN BREADS
The Book of SANDWICHES
The Book of GRILLING & BARBECUES
The Book of SALADS
The Book of DRESSINGS & MARINADES
The Book of CURRIES & INDIAN FOODS
The Book of SOUPS
The Book of CHRISTMAS FOODS
The Book of BREAKFASTS & BRUNCHES

CONTENTS

INTRODUCTION

There can be no doubt about desserts – they are the crowning glory to a meal; the final expression of the thought and care you have taken in preparation and cooking. Whether you serve a homely Bread & Butter Pudding or an exotic Choc Chestnut Gâteau, you can be sure that it will be greeted with delight by all at the table.

There are desserts for everybody and every season in this delicious collection. Such all-time favourites as Queen of Puddings, Pancakes, Oeufs à la Neige and Strawberry Milk Jelly will bring a smile to the faces of all children, and many a grown-up too! For an elegant lunch or dinner party, choose from such classics as Crème Brûlée, Charlotte Russe, Dacquoise or Hot Chocolate Soufflé, or delight your guests with something a little more unusual such as Framboise Zabaglione, Grapefruit Cheesecake or Walnut Gâteau.

Many of the desserts in this book are extremely economical as well as quick and easy to make, while others, for those special occasions, require a little more time and costly ingredients. You can really let your imagination run riot decorating desserts: many of the quick desserts can be turned into party puddings simply by decorating them with rosettes of whipped cream, crystallized fruits, sugar flowers or edible flowers from the garden. Or lift an everyday pudding into the realms of the special by serving it with one of the delicious sauces from the sauce chapter. Desserts are the gastronomic luxuries that make eating really worthwhile – don't ignore them!

TANGERINE SYLLABUB

grated peel and juice of 3 tangerines
grated peel and juice of 1 lemon
90 g (3 oz/⅓ cup) caster sugar
90 ml (3 fl oz/⅓ cup) cream sherry
315 ml (10 fl oz/1 ¼ cups) double (thick) cream
extra grated peel, to decorate, if desired

Put tangerine and lemon peel and both juices into a bowl with sugar and sherry and leave to infuse in a cool place for at least 1 hour.

In a large bowl, whip the cream while gradually pouring in the infused mixture. Keep whipping until mixture is thick enough to form soft peaks.

Pour mixture into a glass serving bowl or individual glasses and chill for at least 2 hours before serving. Decorate with extra peel, if desired.

Serves 4-6.

Note: Use a sharp grater to grate the peel of tangerines, otherwise the peel tends to tear. Warm citrus fruits slightly before squeezing and they will yield more juice.

— STRAWBERRIES ROMANOFF —

750 g (1½ lb) fresh strawberries, hulled
grated peel of 1 orange
4 teaspoons Grand Marnier
315 ml (10 fl oz/1¼ cups) whipping cream
2 tablespoons crème fraîche
1-2 tablespoons icing sugar
langues de chat or round biscuits, to serve

Reserve 4 strawberries for decoration and slice the remainder into a bowl. Add orange peel and Grand Marnier, gently mix together, then leave to macerate for 15 minutes.

In a bowl, whip the cream until quite stiff and fold in the crème fraîche. Sift icing sugar over cream and fold in. Put a spoonful of macerated strawberries into 4 glasses. Mash the remaining strawberries gently and fold into the whipped cream mixture.

Carefully spoon the mixture over the strawberries in the glasses and chill in the refrigerator until ready to serve. Decorate each glass with one of the reserved strawberries cut into a fan shape. Serve with langues de chat or round biscuits.

Serves 4.

Note: Do not hull strawberries until ready to use them.

CRÈME BRÛLÉE

4 egg yolks
2½ teaspoons caster sugar
pinch of cornflour
625 ml (20 fl oz/2½ cups) whipping cream
2 vanilla pods
frosted flowers, to decorate, if desired

CARAMEL TOPPING: caster sugar

In a large bowl, beat egg yolks lightly with sugar and cornflour.

Put cream into a saucepan. With a sharp knife, split open vanilla pods and scrape seeds into cream. Bring almost to boiling point, then pour onto yolks, beating all the time. Pour into top of a double boiler, or a bowl set over a pan of simmering water, and cook over medium heat until mixture thickens sufficiently to coat the back of spoon. Pour into shallow gratin dish. Leave to cool, then chill in the refrigerator overnight.

Two hours before serving, heat grill to very high. Cover surface of pudding thickly and evenly with sugar and place under grill until the sugar has caramellized. Chill for 2 hours. Decorate with frosted flowers, if desired.

Serves 4-6.

Note: The best vanilla pods are coated in white crystals and are very expensive. All vanilla pods can be washed after use and used again. Store them in a dry place.

PINEAPPLE CREAM

3 slices fresh pineapple
440 g (14 oz) can evaporated milk, well chilled
2 teaspoons powdered gelatine
juice of ½ lemon
caster sugar, to taste

TO DECORATE: crystallized pineapple
crystallized angelica

Cut away all skin and 'eyes' from pineapple and cut out core. Purée the flesh in a blender or food processor.

In a bowl, whip evaporated milk until thick and creamy. Sprinkle gelatine over lemon juice in a small bowl and leave to soften for 2-3 minutes. Stand bowl in a saucepan of hot water and stir until the gelatine has dissolved. Stir it into the whipped milk.

Fold pineapple purée into whipped milk and sweeten to taste with sugar. Pour into a glass serving bowl or individual glasses and chill until set. Decorate with crystallized pineapple and angelica cut into leaf shapes just before serving.

Serves 4.

VANILLA BAVAROIS

375 ml (12 fl oz/1½ cups) milk
1 vanilla pod or 3 drops vanilla essence
3 egg yolks
30 g (1 oz/5 teaspoons) caster sugar
3 teaspoons powdered gelatine
pinch of grated nutmeg, if desired
185 ml (6 fl oz/¾ cup) whipping cream
Blackcurrant Sauce (see page 112) or Dark Chocolate
    Sauce (see page 117), to serve
grated chocolate, to decorate, if desired

Put milk and vanilla pod or essence into a saucepan and bring almost to boiling point. Remove from heat.

In a bowl, beat egg yolks and sugar until thick and mousse-like. Pour hot milk onto mixture, beating all the time. Return to saucepan, and stir over low heat until mixture has thickened sufficiently to coat back of spoon. Set aside. Sprinkle gelatine over 5 tablespoons water in a small bowl and leave to soften for 2-3 minutes. Stand bowl in a saucepan of hot water and stir until the gelatine has dissolved. Add to milk mixture, stirring well, then leave to cool, stirring occasionally.

When mixture is on point of setting, add grated nutmeg, if using. Whip cream lightly and fold into mixture. Spoon into a lightly oiled 940 ml (30 fl oz/3¾ cup) mould and refrigerate until set. Turn out and serve with sauce. Decorate with chocolate, if desired.

Serves 4-6.

Variations: Make the bavarois in individual moulds. For Lemon Bavarois, dissolve gelatine in juice of 1 large lemon instead of water and add lemon peel.

CITRUS FLUMMERY

75 ml (2½ fl oz/⅓ cup) frozen concentrated orange and
    passion fruit juice
315 ml (10 fl oz/1¼ cups) double (thick) cream
1 egg white
30 g (1 oz/5 teaspoons) caster sugar (see Note)
orange wedges and passion fruit, to decorate
langues de chat biscuits, to serve

Thaw concentrated fruit juice and measure
out required quantity. (Use remainder as a
drink, making up with water.) In a bowl,
whip cream to soft peaks.

Add juice gradually, continuing to whip
cream, until fairly thick.

In a separate bowl, whisk egg white until stiff.
Whisk in sugar, then fold into creamy
mixture. Spoon into individual glasses and
chill for 1 hour. Decorate with orange wedges
and passion fruit. Serve with the biscuits.

Serves 4-6.

Note: Flavour the sugar for this and other
desserts and cakes by keeping it in a jar with a
vanilla pod. This will give the sugar a strong
vanilla flavour.

GOOSEBERRY ICE CREAM

750 g (1½ lb) gooseberries, thawed if frozen
125 g (4 oz/½ cup) caster sugar
3 egg yolks
1 small avocado
315 ml (10 fl oz/1¼ cups) whipping cream
gooseberries, leaves or borage flowers, to decorate, if
   desired

Put gooseberries into a saucepan with 2 tablespoons water and cook over a low heat until soft. Purée in a blender or food processor, then sieve to remove pips. Set aside to cool.

Put sugar into a saucepan with 2 tablespoons water, dissolve over medium heat, then boil syrup to thread stage, 110C (225F) on a sugar thermometer. In a bowl, beat egg yolks lightly, then pour syrup onto them and whisk until mixture is thick and mousse-like. Peel avocado, discard stone and mash flesh. Mix into gooseberry purée. Whip cream and fold into egg mixture with purée. Turn into rigid plastic container and freeze for 1-2 hours until beginning to be firm.

Remove from freezer and beat well. Freeze until firm. Transfer to refrigerator to soften for 30 minutes before serving. Serve in scoops in chilled glasses. Decorate each one with gooseberries, leaves or borage flowers.

Serves 4-6.

Note: Avocado gives this ice-cream a lovely texture. Its taste is not discernible.
   When cooking acidic fruits, such as gooseberries, do not use an aluminium pan. The fruit will taste metallic.

NUTTY BROWN BREAD CREAM

60 g (2 oz/½ cup) hazelnuts
75 g (2½ oz/1¼ cups) fresh brown breadcrumbs
30 g (1 oz/2 tablespoons) demerara sugar
2 egg whites
90 g (3 oz/⅓ cup) caster sugar
315 ml (10 fl oz/1¼ cups) whipping cream
1-2 drops vanilla essence

Toast hazelnuts evenly, cool, then grind coarsely in a coffee grinder. Mix with breadcrumbs and demerara sugar in a bowl.

Tip crumb mixture onto a baking sheet and spread out evenly. Grill under medium-hot grill, turning and shaking, until brown. Leave to cool. Whisk egg whites in a large bowl, until stiff. Sprinkle in sugar and whisk for a further 2 minutes. In a separate bowl, whip cream with vanilla essence to soft peaks, then fold into egg whites with all but 1 tablespoon of breadcrumb mixture.

Spoon mixture into 6 glasses and chill until ready to serve. Sprinkle with reserved crumb mixture just before serving.

Serves 6.

Note: This mixture makes a delicious ice cream; simply turn the finished cream into a plastic container and freeze.

ROSE CREAM

625 ml (20 fl oz/2½ cups) whipping cream
3 teaspoons powdered gelatine
5-6 teaspoons triple strength rosewater
grated peel and juice of 1 lemon
60 g (2 oz/¼ cup) caster sugar

ROSE PETALS: **1 egg white**
petals from 1 rose
caster sugar

To prepare rose petals, preheat oven to 110C (225F/Gas ¼). Whisk egg white until frothy and dip rose petals in to cover.

Toss petals in caster sugar and place on baking tray covered with silicone paper. Bake in the bottom of oven for about 2½ hours, leaving oven door slightly ajar, until dry and hard. Place all ingredients for cream in a heavy-based saucepan and stir over a very low heat until gelatine and sugar have dissolved. Do not allow to boil.

Pour into 6 ramekin dishes and cool at room temperature. Chill creams in refrigerator until ready to serve, then decorate with the frosted rose petals.

Serves 6.

Note: The rose petals can be prepared in advance and stored in an airtight tin. For extra colour, decorate with frosted rose leaves as well as petals but do not eat them.

— CREAMY CRANBERRY FOOL —

185 g (6 oz) cranberries, fresh or frozen, thawed if
 frozen
90 ml (3 fl oz/⅓ cup) orange juice
185 g (6 oz/¾ cup) caster sugar
315 ml (10 fl oz/1¼ cups) whipping cream
grated orange peel, to decorate

Put cranberries into a saucepan with orange
juice and sugar and simmer for about 10
minutes, until berries pop. Set aside to cool.

When cranberries are cold, rub through a fine
metal sieve, using a wooden spoon. In a large
bowl, whip cream until stiff and fold in purée.
Chill until ready to serve.

Serve fool in individual glasses topped with a
little grated orange peel.

Serves 4.

Note: Substitute 250 g (8 oz) damson for the
cranberries. Cook them with 3 tablespoons
water and omit orange juice.

CABINET PUDDING

60 g (2 oz/⅓ cup) raisins
2 tablespoons rum, brandy or water
315 g (10 oz) chocolate or plain sponge cake
125 g (4 oz/½ cup) caster sugar
125 g (4 oz/1 cup) chopped mixed nuts
4 eggs
500 ml (16 fl oz/2 cups) milk
30 g (1 oz/¼ cup) flaked almonds
raspberries, to decorate
Raspberry Sauce (see page 115), to serve

Soak raisins in rum, brandy or water for at least 1 hour. Meanwhile, preheat oven to 180C (350F/Gas 4). Lightly butter a 1.25 litre (40 fl oz/5 cup) pie dish.

Roughly break up sponge cake and put into prepared pie dish. Add raisins and soaking liquid, then sprinkle with just over one-quarter of sugar and all chopped mixed nuts. In a bowl, beat eggs with remaining sugar and whisk in milk. Pour into pie dish. Scatter with flaked almonds.

Put pie dish into a roasting tin and add enough boiling water to come halfway up sides. Bake in the oven for 1-1½ hours, until lightly set. Decorate with raspberries and serve hot with Raspberry Sauce.

Serves 6.

Note: Stale, leftover sponge is ideal for this pudding, or ratafias can be used in place of sponge cake, if preferred.

—— ALMOND BLANCMANGE ——

90 g (3 oz/½ cup) whole blanched almonds
4 egg yolks
125 g (4 oz/½ cup) caster sugar
375 ml (12 fl oz/1½ cups) milk
3 teaspoons powdered gelatine
250 ml (8 fl oz/1 cup) whipping cream
toasted flaked almonds and herb sprigs, to decorate

Toast whole blanched almonds, turning frequently to brown evenly. Cool and grind coarsely in a coffee grinder or food processor.

In a bowl, beat egg yolks and sugar until thick and mousse-like. Put milk into a saucepan and bring almost to boiling point. Beat into egg mixture. Return to saucepan, and stir over low heat until mixture has thickened sufficiently to coat the back of the spoon. Do not boil. Remove from heat and leave to cool. Sprinkle gelatine over 3 tablespoons water in a small bowl and leave to soften for 2-3 minutes. Stand bowl in a saucepan of hot water and stir until gelatine has dissolved. Stir into milk mixture.

In another bowl, whip cream lightly. When milk mixture is on point of setting, stir in ground almonds and fold in cream. Spoon into a serving dish or individual glasses and chill until set. When ready to serve, decorate with toasted flaked almonds and herb sprigs.

Serves 6.

Note: Grind whole nuts rather than buying them ready ground for the best flavour. Toasting them helps to bring out the flavour still further.

STRAWBERRY MILK JELLY

500 ml (16 fl oz/2 cups) strawberry-flavoured drinking
  yogurt
3 teaspoons powdered gelatine
250 g (8 oz) strawberries

Pour yogurt into a bowl and chill.

Sprinkle gelatine over 3 tablespoons water in
a small bowl and leave to soften for 2-3
minutes. Stand the bowl in a saucepan of hot
water and stir until the gelatine has dissolved.
Whisk into chilled yogurt, then pour into a
dampened 625 ml (20 fl oz/2½ cup) mould.
Leave to set.

When ready to serve, slice strawberries. Turn
out mould onto a serving plate and surround
with strawberries.

Serves 4.

Note: For a softer texture jelly, increase
quantity of yogurt to 625 ml (20 fl oz/2½
cups), but set in a bowl rather than a mould.

Variation: The jelly can be made in
individual moulds, if preferred.

— MAPLE BAVARIAN CREAM —

1 ½ teaspoons powdered gelatine
3 tablespoons lemon juice and water, mixed
315 ml (10 fl oz/1 ¼ cups) double (thick) cream
5 tablespoons maple syrup
90 g (3 oz) crème fraîche
extra maple syrup for serving
langues de chat biscuits, to serve

Sprinkle gelatine over lemon juice and water in a small bowl and leave to soften for 2-3 minutes. In a bowl, whip cream lightly, adding half the maple syrup.

Stand gelatine bowl in a saucepan of hot water and stir until the gelatine has dissolved. Stir in remaining maple syrup, then pour into the cream, and whisk again until cream stands in soft peaks.

Fold crème fraîche into maple cream mixture. Spoon into individual glasses and chill until set. Top with extra maple syrup and serve with langues de chat biscuits.

Serves 4.

Note: Real maple syrup, as opposed to maple-flavoured syrup, is very expensive and not always easy to obtain. It is worth seeking out for this pudding, as it greatly improves the flavour of the cream.

COEURS À LA CRÈME

250 g (8 oz) ricotta or cottage cheese
30 g (1 oz/5 teaspoons) caster sugar
1 teaspoon lemon juice
315 ml (10 fl oz/1¼ cups) double (thick) cream
2 egg whites

TO SERVE: **fresh fruit or Raspberry Sauce (see page 115)**
double (thick) cream

Line 8 heart-shaped moulds with muslin. Press cheese through a sieve into a bowl. Stir in sugar and lemon juice.

In a separate bowl, whip cream until stiff. Stir into cheese mixture. Whisk egg whites until stiff, then fold into the cheese mixture.

Spoon into moulds, place on 2 plates and leave to drain overnight in the refrigerator. To serve, unmould onto individual plates and gently remove the muslin. Serve the hearts with fresh fruit with cream handed separately, or with whipped cream and Raspberry Sauce.

Serves 8.

Note: To add extra colour, decorate with sprigs of redcurrants and blackcurrants.

— ORANGE CARAMEL CREAM —

125 g (4 oz/½ cup) granulated sugar
3 eggs
8 teaspoons caster sugar
315 ml (10 fl oz/1¼ cups) milk
3 teaspoons sweet orange oil
1 orange
fresh herbs, to decorate

Preheat oven to 180C (350F/Gas 4). Warm 4 china ramekin dishes or 4 dariole moulds. Put granulated sugar and 3 tablespoons water into a small saucepan and place over a low heat to dissolve sugar. Increase heat and boil steadily, without stirring, to a rich brown caramel.

Divide between the dishes or moulds, tipping them to cover bottom and sides with caramel. Set aside. In a bowl, beat eggs and caster sugar together. Heat milk until almost boiling, then pour over egg mixture, beating all the time. Stir in orange oil.

Strain mixture into dishes or moulds. Grate orange peel finely, divide between dishes and stir in. Place dishes in a roasting tin, pour in boiling water to come halfway up the sides, then bake in the oven for about 20 minutes, until set. Cool in the dishes, then chill until required. Turn out onto serving plates, and decorate with segments cut from the grated orange and herb leaves.

Serves 4.

AMARETTI MOUSSE

100 g (3½ oz/½ cup) whole blanched almonds
60 g (2 oz) amaretti biscuits
3 eggs, plus 2 extra yolks
90 g (3 oz/⅓ cup) caster sugar
3 teaspoons powdered gelatine
2 tablespoons lemon juice
1-2 tablespoons Amaretto or kirsch
315 ml (10 fl oz/1¼ cups) whipping cream

Toast nuts under a medium grill to brown. Put with biscuits in food processor fitted with metal blade and process to crumbs.

In a bowl, whisk eggs, extra yolks and sugar together until thick and mousse-like. Sprinkle gelatine over lemon juice in a small bowl and leave to soften for 2-3 minutes. Stand bowl in saucepan of hot water and stir until gelatine has dissolved. Add to egg mixture with liqueur and three-quarters of nut and biscuit mixture. Whip cream stiffly and fold two-thirds into mixture.

Pour mixture into a 1 litre (32 fl oz/ 4 cup) soufflé dish and put in refrigerator to set. Just before serving, decorate with piped rosettes of reserved whipping cream and sprinkle remaining nuts and biscuits on top.

Serves 6-8.

Note: Amaretto is a very sweet liqueur made from almonds. Kirsch gives a more subtle flavour and makes the dessert less sweet.

BANANA BRÛLÉE

625 ml (20 fl oz/2½ cups) whipping cream
3 large bananas
juice of 1 small lemon
60 g (2 oz/¼ cup) caster sugar
few crumbled meringues (see page 36), if desired
125 g (4 oz/½ cup) granulated sugar

In a large bowl, whip cream until thick. Slice bananas thinly into a separate bowl and toss in lemon juice.

Fold bananas and caster sugar into whipped cream with crumbled meringues, if using. Spoon the mixture into a serving dish and place in the refrigerator.

Put granulated sugar and 1 tablespoon water into a small saucepan and place over a low heat to dissolve sugar. Do not stir. When sugar has dissolved, increase heat and boil syrup to a rich brown caramel. Immediately dribble this over banana cream mixture, then replace in refrigerator for caramel to harden. Serve within 1-2 hours.

Serves 6.

CARAMEL RICE

75 g (2½ oz/⅓ cup) pudding rice, washed and drained
625 ml (20 fl oz/2½ cups) milk
1 vanilla pod
125 ml (4 fl oz/½ cup) single (light) cream
juice of 1 orange
caster sugar
orange peel strips, to decorate

Put rice, milk and vanilla pod into a saucepan and simmer on a very low heat for 45-60 minutes, until rice is soft and creamy.

Remove vanilla pod from mixture and stir in cream and orange juice. Spoon into an ovenproof gratin or soufflé dish. Leave to go cold, then refrigerate until ready to serve.

Cover top of pudding thickly and evenly with caster sugar. Place under a very hot grill until sugar topping has caramellized. Serve at once, decorated with orange peel.

Serves 4.

Note: Chill the pudding again before serving, if preferred, but serve within 2 hours.

QUEEN OF PUDDINGS

500 ml (16 fl oz/2 cups) milk
155 ml (5 fl oz/²⁄₃ cup) single cream
grated peel of 1 small lemon
90 g (3 oz/1½ cups) fresh white breadcrumbs
45 g (1½ oz/9 teaspoons) butter
250 g (8 oz/1¼ cups) caster sugar
3 small eggs, separated
3 tablespoons raspberry jam

Preheat oven to 180C (350F/Gas 4). Butter a 1.25 litre (40 fl oz/5 cup) pie dish. Put milk, cream and lemon peel in a saucepan.

Heat milk mixture gently for 5 minutes, then remove from heat and leave to infuse for 5 minutes. Put breadcrumbs, butter and one-quarter of the sugar into a bowl and pour the warm milk on top. Stir until butter and sugar have dissolved. In a small bowl, beat egg yolks, then stir them into breadcrumb mixture. Turn into prepared pie dish and bake for 45-50 minutes, until set. Remove from oven and cool slightly. Warm raspberry jam in a pan and spread over pudding.

Lower oven temperature to 160C (325F/Gas 3). In a large bowl, whisk egg whites until stiff, then fold in remaining sugar. Pile this meringue mixture onto pudding and return to oven for about 20 minutes, until meringue is crisp and golden. Serve warm or cold.

Serves 4.

Note: Sieve the warmed raspberry jam to remove pips, if desired.

— BREAD & BUTTER PUDDING —

125 g (4 oz/¾ cup) sultanas and currants, mixed
8 slices thin white bread, buttered
30 g (1 oz/2 tablespoons) candied fruit, chopped
caster sugar for sprinkling

CUSTARD: 1 egg yolk
315 ml (10 fl oz/1¼ cups) milk
155 ml (5 fl oz/⅔ cup) single (light) cream
1 vanilla pod
1 teaspoon caster sugar

Put sultanas and currants into a bowl and cover with water. Leave to swell. Preheat oven to 180C (350F/Gas 4). Grease a 1 litre (32 fl oz/4 cup) pie dish.

Cut crusts from bread and sandwich 4 slices together. Cut into 6 pieces and place in prepared pie dish. Drain fruit and scatter over bread with chopped candied fruit. Top with remaining bread, butter side up.

Put egg yolk in a medium bowl. Put milk, cream, vanilla pod and sugar into a saucepan and bring almost to boiling point. Pour over egg, stir, then strain into pie dish, pouring down sides so top slices of bread are not soaked. Stand for 30 minutes, then sprinkle with caster sugar and place in a roasting tin. Pour in boiling water to come halfway up sides of dish and bake in the oven for 45-50 minutes, until top is golden brown.

Serves 4.

— GRAPEFRUIT CHEESECAKE —

250 g (8 oz) semi-sweet wheatmeal biscuits
125 g (4 oz/½ cup) butter, melted
2 pink grapefruit
3 teaspoons powdered gelatine
250 g (8 oz) cream cheese
155 ml (5 fl oz/⅔ cup) single (light) cream
2 tablespoons caster sugar
juice and grated peel of 1 lemon
4 egg whites

Crush biscuits to crumbs and mix with the melted butter.

Press two-thirds of the crumb mixture over base of a 22.5 cm (9 in) loose-bottomed or springform tin and chill. Cut off peel and pith from grapefruit, holding over a bowl to catch juice. Cut out segments from between membranes and set aside. Squeeze membranes into bowl to extract juice. Sprinkle gelatine over grapefruit juice and leave for 2-3 minutes to soften. Stand in a saucepan of hot water and stir until gelatine has dissolved. In a bowl, beat cream cheese, cream and sugar. Stir in gelatine, lemon juice and peel.

Whisk egg whites in a large bowl until stiff. Fold into creamy mixture. Pour over crumb mixture and return tin to refrigerator to set. To serve, remove cheesecake from tin and decorate with grapefruit segments. Press remaining crumbs evenly into sides of cake.

Serves 6-8.

Note: If liked, salt can be sprinkled onto the grapefruit to act as an alkali, making the grapefruit less acidic, so less sugar is needed to sweeten the fruit.

COFFEE BOMBE

3 eggs, separated
185 g (6 oz/¾ cup) caster sugar
75 ml (2½ fl oz/⅓ cup) cold strong black coffee
500 ml (16 fl oz/2 cups) double (thick) cream
155 g (5 oz) meringues
whipped cream and chocolate coffee beans, to decorate
hot Bitter Mocha Sauce (see page 118)

In a large bowl, beat egg yolks and sugar together until thick and mousse-like. Gently stir in coffee. In a separate bowl, whip cream lightly. Crush meringues.

Fold cream and meringues into coffee mixture. In a large bowl, whisk egg whites until stiff and fold 1 tablespoon into coffee mixture. Tip egg whites onto coffee mixture, then fold together carefully. Pour into a 2 litre (64 fl oz/8 cup) lightly oiled bombe mould and freeze until firm.

One hour before serving, transfer the bombe to the refrigerator to soften slightly. Turn out onto a serving dish and decorate with cream and chocolate coffee beans. Serve with hot Bitter Mocha Sauce handed separately.

Serves 8.

Note: To turn out bombe, wring out a tea-towel in very hot water and wrap it around the mould. Invert onto a serving plate and lift off mould.

CHARLOTTE RUSSE

16 sponge fingers
3 teaspoons powdered gelatine
4 egg yolks
90 g (3 oz/⅓ cup) caster sugar
625 ml (20 fl oz/2½ cups) whipping cream
1 vanilla pod, split open
315 ml (10 fl oz/1¼ cups) thick sour cream
185 g (6 oz) fresh raspberries
whipped cream, to decorate

Line the base of 1.1 litre (35 fl oz/4¼ cup) charlotte mould with greaseproof paper. Stand sponge fingers, pressing against each other, round sides of mould and trim to fit.

Sprinkle gelatine over 3 tablespoons of water in a small bowl and leave to soften for 2-3 minutes. In a bowl, whisk egg yolks and sugar together until thick and mousse-like. Put 375 ml (12 fl oz/1½ cups) whipping cream in a saucepan with vanilla pod and bring almost to boiling point. Strain over egg mixture, stirring well. Pour back into saucepan and stir over low heat until mixture has thickened slightly. Do not boil.

Strain into clean bowl and add soaked gelatine. Stir until dissolved. Cool, then stand bowl in larger bowl of iced water and stir until mixture thickens. Whip remaining cream with sour cream and fold into mixture. Pour into prepared mould, cover with plastic wrap and refrigerate overnight. When ready to serve, turn out onto serving plate, remove greaseproof paper and decorate with the raspberries and whipped cream. Tie a ribbon round pudding.

Serves 6-8.

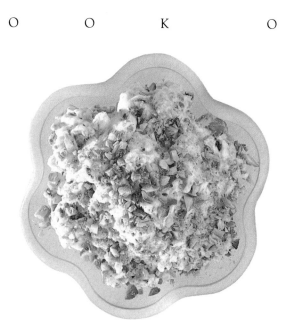

ATHOLL BROSE

45 g (1½ oz/3 tablespoons) medium oatmeal
60 g (2 oz/⅓ cup) whole blanched almonds
315 ml (10 fl oz/1¼ cups) double (thick) cream
60 ml (2 fl oz/¼ cup) whisky
90 g (3 oz/¼ cup) orange flower honey
1 tablespoon lemon juice

Toast oatmeal under a medium-hot grill until evenly browned. Toast the almonds in the same way, then chop them finely.

In a large bowl, whip cream to soft peaks, then gradually whisk in whisky, honey and lemon juice.

Fold oatmeal and half the chopped almonds into creamy mixture and spoon into 4 glasses. Chill in the refrigerator. When ready to serve, sprinkle remaining almonds on top of each pudding.

Serves 4.

Note: This traditional Scottish dessert is very rich and is perfect for a dinner party.

—— YOGURT FUDGE CREAM ——

315 ml (10 fl oz/1 ¼ cups) whipping cream
250 g (8 oz/1 cup) natural yogurt
250 g (8 oz/1 ½ cups) brown sugar
fresh strawberries or raspberries, to serve, if desired

In a large bowl, whip cream to stiff peaks. Fold in the yogurt.

Half fill 4 glasses with the creamy mixture. Sprinkle with about one-third of the sugar. Spoon remaining creamy mixture on top of the sugar, then pile on remaining sugar.

Chill in the refrigerator overnight. Serve puddings on their own, or with fresh strawberries or raspberries, if desired.

Serves 4.

Note: The brown sugar dissolves and forms a fudgy layer in these puddings. They must be prepared a day in advance to allow for this.

OEUFS À LA NEIGE

4 eggs, separated
scant ½ teaspoon cornflour
90 g (3 oz/⅓ cup) caster sugar
125 ml (4 fl oz/½ cup) milk
315 ml (10 fl oz/1¼ cups) single (light) cream
1 vanilla pod
1 tablespoon orange flower water
1 tablespoon toasted, flaked almonds
orange peel strips, to decorate

In a bowl, cream egg yolks with cornflour and one-third of the caster sugar. Place milk, cream and vanilla pod in a saucepan and scald (bring to near boiling point).

Pour the hot milk over the egg yolks, whisking all the time. Place bowl over a saucepan of simmering water and cook gently, stirring, until it is the consistency of double cream. Cool, remove vanilla pod and stir in orange flower water. In a large bowl, whisk egg whites until stiff, add remaining sugar and whisk again.

Fill a large saucepan with water and bring to simmering point. Put spoonfuls of meringue mixture, a few at a time, into water and poach for 5 minutes, turning carefully once. (There should be enough meringue for 4 spoonfuls per portion.) Drain on absorbent kitchen paper and cool. Pour most of the custard into a glass serving bowl and arrange meringue puffs on top. Drizzle the remaining custard over meringues, then sprinkle with flaked almonds. Decorate with orange peel.

Serves 4.

RED BERRY SOUFFLÉ

30 g (1 oz/6 teaspoons) butter
125 g (4 oz/½ cup) caster sugar, plus 1 extra tablespoon
250 g (8 oz) mixed soft red fruits, fresh or frozen,
    thawed if frozen
1 tablespoon Fraise liqueur or crème de cassis
5 egg whites
icing sugar, to serve

Preheat oven to 180C (350F/Gas 4). Use the butter to grease a 1 litre (32 fl oz/4 cup) soufflé dish or 6 individual dishes, then dust out with 1 tablespoon caster sugar.

Purée fruit, liqueur and remaining caster sugar together in a blender or food processor. Turn into a bowl. In a separate bowl, whisk egg whites until stiff, but not dry. Fold 1 tablespoon into fruit purée, then tip purée onto whites and fold together carefully, using a metal spoon.

Spoon mixture into prepared soufflé dish, place on a baking sheet and bake in the oven for 25-30 minutes for the large soufflé; 15-20 minutes for the individual soufflés, until risen and just set. Dust with a little icing sugar and serve immediately.

Serves 6.

— MERINGUES WITH HONEY —

2 egg whites
125 g (4 oz/½ cup) caster sugar

TO SERVE: 2 tablespoons clear honey
2 tablespoons toasted flaked almonds
315 ml (10 fl oz/1¼ cups) whipping cream

Preheat oven to 150C (300F/Gas 2). Line baking sheets with silicone paper. Put egg whites into a large bowl and whisk until stiff, but not dry.

Sprinkle 1 tablespoon sugar over egg whites and whisk for 1 minute more. Sprinkle half the remaining sugar over the mixture and fold in carefully, using a metal spoon. Then fold in remaining sugar. Spoon meringue into a piping bag fitted with a plain or star nozzle and pipe 12-16 small circles or ovals onto prepared sheets. Alternatively, simply place spoonfuls of meringue onto prepared sheets.

Bake meringues in the oven for 1-1½ hours, until crisp on the outside. Cool on a wire rack. When cold, pile onto a serving plate, dribble honey over the top and sprinkle with toasted flaked almonds. Whip cream until stiff and serve separately.

Makes 12-16 shells.

Note: An electric or hand whisk can be used to make meringues. Separate eggs carefully so there is no yolk with the white.

CHOCOLATE MERINGUES

1 quantity of Meringue mixture (see left)
125 g (4 oz) plain (dark) chocolate
315 ml (10 fl oz/1¼ cups) whipping cream
fresh strawberries, hulled, to decorate

Preheat oven to 150C (300F/Gas 2). Line 2 baking sheets with silicone paper. Use meringue mixture to pipe 12 shells onto prepared baking sheets. Cook and cool as described (see left).

Break chocolate into squares and melt with 2 tablespoons water in the top of a double boiler or a bowl set over a saucepan of simmering water. Stir occasionally, until melted and smooth. Dip the flat underside of meringues into melted chocolate to cover. Set on their sides for the chocolate to harden.

Whip cream, place in piping bag fitted with a star nozzle and pipe onto 6 shells. Sandwich in pairs with remaining 6 shells. Place meringues in paper serving cases, or on individual plates, and decorate with slices of strawberries.

Serves 6.

Note: A few drops of red food colouring can be added to basic meringue mixture to colour it pink, if desired.

MINI PAVLOVAS

2 egg whites
345 g (11 oz/1½ cups) caster sugar
½ teaspoon vinegar
½ teaspoon cornflour
4 tablespoons boiling water

TO SERVE: 1 quantity of Citrus Flummery (see page 13)
   or whipped cream and Blackcurrant Sauce (see
   page 112)
orange peel, if desired

Preheat oven to 120C (250F/Gas ½). Line 2 baking sheets with silicone paper. In a large bowl, stir together egg whites, sugar, vinegar and cornflour.

Add boiling water and whisk with an electric whisk until mixture is white and thick – this takes a good 10 minutes. Place 8 large spoonfuls on the prepared baking sheets and spread out to 10 cm (4 in) diameter circles. Make a slight depression in the centre of each, using the back of a spoon.

Bake pavlovas in the oven for about 30 minutes, until crisp on the outside – they are like marshmallow on the inside. Remove from baking sheets and cool on wire trays. For serving, fill the centres with Citrus Flummery, spooning or piping it into the pavlovas. Alternatively, fill with whipped cream with Blackcurrant Sauce poured over the top. Decorate with orange peel cut into shapes, if desired.

Serves 8.

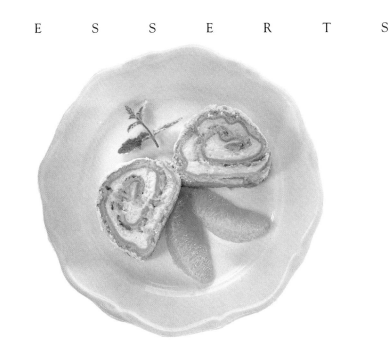

— ORANGE ROULADE —

5 eggs, separated
185 g (6 oz/¾ cup) caster sugar, plus extra to sweeten
 cream
grated peel and juice of 2 oranges
icing sugar
315 ml (10 fl oz/1¼ cups) whipping cream
fresh orange segments, to decorate
Raspberry Sauce (see page 115), to serve, if desired

Preheat oven to 180C (350F/Gas 4). Line a swiss roll tin with double thickness foil and grease very well. In a bowl, whisk egg yolks, sugar and orange peel until thick.

In a large bowl, whisk egg whites until stiff but not dry. Fold 1 tablespoon into egg yolk mixture, then tip egg yolk mixture onto whites and fold together carefully. Pour into prepared tin and spread evenly. Bake in the oven for 30 minutes, remove from oven and immediately cover with a damp tea towel. When quite cold, turn onto a piece of foil thickly dusted with icing sugar. Peel off bottom layer of foil, in long, thin strips.

In a bowl, whip cream lightly and sweeten to taste. Gradually add orange juice, whisking all the time, until stiff. Reserve a little cream for decoration and spread remainder evenly over sponge. Roll up, using the foil to help and transfer to a serving plate. Pipe rosettes along sides using reserved cream and decorate with fresh orange segments. Serve with Raspberry Sauce, if using.

Serves 6.

PANCAKES

125 g (4 oz/1 cup) plain flour
pinch of salt
1 egg, plus 1 extra egg yolk
315 ml (10 fl oz/1¼ cups) milk
2 tablespoons oil or melted butter

TO SERVE: lemon wedges
caster sugar

Sift flour and salt onto a plate. Put into a food processor with egg, egg yolk and half the milk. Blend well, then add remaining milk and oil or melted butter and blend again. Stand for 30 minutes.

To make batter by hand, sift flour and salt into large bowl, make a well in the centre. Beat egg, egg yolk and half the milk together and tip into well. Using a wooden spoon, gradually stir flour into liquid, keeping batter smooth. Add remaining milk and beat well until bubbles appear round surface of batter. Leave to stand for 30 minutes – this allows flour to swell. Beat again before using.

Heat a 15-17.5 cm (6-7 in) heavy-based frying pan and grease lightly. Pour in just enough batter to cover bottom of pan. Cook over medium heat for 1-2 minutes, until underside is lightly browned. Turn or toss pancake and cook other side for same amount of time. Turn out and keep warm while cooking remaining pancakes. Serve sprinkled with lemon juice and sugar.

Serves 4.

CRÊPE RIBBONS

1 quantity of Pancakes (see left)
oil for deep frying

TO SERVE: icing sugar
Raspberry Sauce, Blackcurrant Sauce or Crème à la
Vanille (see pages 115, 112, and 114)

Leave the cooked pancakes to cool.

Cut cold pancakes into ribbons or strips.
Heat a pan of oil for deep frying; test the
temperature by dropping in a small piece of
pancake. It should sizzle furiously. Fry the
ribbons in batches, until crisp and golden.
Remove with a slotted spoon and drain on
crumpled absorbent kitchen paper. Keep
warm while cooking the remainder.

Pile the warm crêpe ribbons onto a serving
dish, dredge with icing sugar and serve
immediately with chosen sauce.

Serves 4.

Note: Pancakes for this recipe can be made a
day in advance and kept, wrapped in foil, in
the refrigerator, or they may be frozen. Thaw
the pancakes for 1-2 hours at room
temperature before frying.

APPLE PANCAKES

125 g (4 oz/1 cup) plain flour
pinch of salt
250 ml (8 fl oz/1 cup) milk and water, mixed
2 eggs
1 tablespoon oil
3 well-flavoured eating apples
2 teaspoons lemon juice
1 tablespoon brandy
2 teaspoons caster sugar

Make pancake batter as described on page 40 and leave to stand for 30 minutes.

Peel and core apples and slice very finely onto a plate. Sprinkle with lemon juice and brandy. Heat a 15-17.5 cm (6-7 in) heavy-based frying pan and grease lightly. Pour in 1 tablespoon batter and roll pan to spread it evenly. Put a few apple slices over pancake, then spoon a little more batter over apple. Cook for 2-3 minutes, until batter is almost set. Hold pan under a hot grill to finish cooking batter.

Turn pancake out onto a plate and serve as soon as possible, sprinkled with a little caster sugar. Continue until all the batter is used.

Serves 4.

Note: Mixing water with the milk helps to lighten pancake batter. Beer or cider can be used instead of milk.

PASSION FRUIT MOUSSE

12 passion fruit
juice and grated peel of 1 large orange
5 eggs
125 g (4 oz/½ cup) caster sugar
3 teaspoons powdered gelatine
315 ml (10 fl oz/1¼ cups) whipping cream

Cut passion fruit in half, scoop out flesh and place in a saucepan with orange juice. Heat gently for 2-3 minutes, cool and then chill in the refrigerator.

In a large bowl, whisk orange peel, eggs and sugar until thick and mousse-like. Sprinkle gelatine over 3 tablespoons water in a small bowl and leave to soften for 2-3 minutes. Stand bowl in a saucepan of hot water and stir until gelatine has dissolved. Add to egg mixture. Sieve chilled passion fruit mixture and stir half into mousse. Return remainder to refrigerator.

In a bowl, whip cream lightly and fold into mousse mixture. Turn into a soufflé dish or glass serving bowl and chill until required. Serve reserved passion fruit mixture separately as a sauce.

Serves 6.

Note: Put passion fruit into a bowl with unripe fruits, and the unripe fruits will ripen more speedily.

FRAMBOISE ZABAGLIONE

4 egg yolks
220 ml (7 fl oz/⅞ cup) Framboise liqueur
30 g (1 oz/5 teaspoons) caster sugar
strawberries or raspberries, to decorate, if desired
langues de chat biscuits, to serve

Put egg yolks, liqueur and sugar into a double boiler or a bowl set over a saucepan of simmering water.

Set over a medium heat and, using a balloon whisk, whisk the mixture until it is very thick and mousse-like in appearance – this will take about 20 minutes.

Pour mixture into glasses, decorate with strawberries or raspberries if desired, and serve immediately, while still warm, with langues de chat biscuits.

Serves 4.

Note: Although it is laborious it is important to use a hand whisk for this recipe. An electric whisk increases the volume of the eggs too quickly, so that they do not have a chance to cook. The mixture will then collapse when it is poured into glasses.

SOUFFLÉ OMELETTE

3 eggs, separated
1 tablespoon single (light) cream
2 teaspoons caster sugar
15 g (½ oz/3 teaspoons) butter
6 teaspoons raspberry jam
icing sugar

Preheat oven to 200C (400F/Gas 6). In a bowl, beat egg yolks, cream and sugar lightly. In a separate larger bowl, whisk egg whites until stiff. Add yolk mixture to whisked whites and carefully fold together.

Melt butter in an omelette pan over medium heat and pour soufflé mixture into pan. Spread it evenly and cook for about 1 minute, until brown underneath. Put pan in oven for 5 minutes, until top is set. Meanwhile, heat 2 skewers either in a gas flame or under a very hot grill until they are red hot and glowing.

In a small saucepan, warm jam slightly. Remove omelette from oven and quickly spread with jam. Fold over and transfer to a serving plate. Sift icing sugar thickly over omelette, then holding the skewers with thick oven gloves, mark a criss-cross pattern in the icing sugar by pressing the skewers into it. Cut omelette in half and serve.

Serves 2.

DACQUOISE

155 g (5 oz/1 cup) whole blanched almonds
5 egg whites
315 g (10 oz/1½ cups) caster sugar
185 g (6 oz/2¾ cups) dried apricots
juice of 1 lemon
375 ml (12 fl oz/1½ cups) whipping cream
toasted flaked almonds, to decorate

Preheat oven to 150C (300F/Gas 2). Line a baking sheet with silicone paper. Toast almonds under a medium grill to brown evenly. Cool, then grind finely in a coffee grinder or food processor. Set aside.

In a large bowl, whisk egg whites until stiff, but not dry. Sprinkle over 2 tablespoons of the caster sugar and whisk for a further 1 minute. Fold in remaining sugar with ground almonds, using a metal spoon. Spoon meringue onto lined baking sheet and spread evenly to a 25 cm (10 in) circle. Bake in the oven for 1½-2 hours, until dry and biscuit coloured. Peel off paper and cool meringue on a wire rack.

Put apricots and lemon juice into a saucepan, cover with water and simmer over medium heat for about 30 minutes, until tender. Cool, then purée apricots with a little cooking liquid in a blender or food processor to make a thick purée. Whip cream stiffly and fold half the purée into it. Pile onto meringue and dribble remaining purée, thinned with a little more cooking liquid, over top. Sprinkle with flaked almonds to decorate.

Serves 6-8.

CHERRY CLAFOUTI

750 g (1½ lb) stoned black cherries, fresh or frozen,
   thawed if frozen
90 g (3 oz/¾ cup) plain flour
pinch of salt
3 eggs
90 g (3 oz/⅓ cup) caster sugar
500 ml (16 fl oz/2 cups) milk
1 tablespoon cherry brandy or kirsch
icing sugar, to serve

Preheat oven to 200C (400F/Gas 6). Drain the cherries, if thawed. Butter a 1.25 litre (40 fl oz/5 cup) pie dish and put cherries in it.

Sift flour and salt together onto a plate. In a large bowl, beat eggs with sugar until creamy, then fold in flour. Warm milk slightly in a saucepan over a low heat and stir into egg mixture with cherry brandy or kirsch. Beat well to make batter smooth, then pour the batter over the cherries.

Bake in the oven for 30 minutes, until batter is set and golden. Serve warm, dusted with icing sugar.

Serves 6.

Note: Fresh cherries can taste a little bland when cooked. Add 1-2 drops almond essence to improve the flavour, if desired.

– MIXED CHOCOLATE TERRINE –

WHITE CHOCOLATE MOUSSE: 280 g (9 oz) white
   chocolate
1 ½ teaspoons powdered gelatine
1 good tablespoon liquid glucose
2 egg yolks
155 ml (5 fl oz/²⁄₃ cup) double (thick) cream
155 ml (5 fl oz/²⁄₃ cup) thick sour cream

DARK CHOCOLATE MOUSSE: 185 g (6 oz) plain (dark)
   chocolate
4 tablespoons strong black coffee
2 teaspoons powdered gelatine
125 g (4 oz/½ cup) butter, cut into cubes
2 egg yolks
315 ml (10 fl oz/1 ¼ cups) whipping cream

Line a 1 kg (2 lb) loaf tin with plastic wrap to
overlap edges. To make the white chocolate
mousse, break the white chocolate into small
pieces and set aside. Sprinkle gelatine over 2
tablespoons water in a small bowl and leave
to soften for 2-3 minutes. Put 3 tablespoons
water in a saucepan with glucose and bring to
the boil. Remove from heat and stir in
gelatine until dissolved. Add chocolate and
beat mixture until chocolate has melted and
is smooth.

Beat in egg yolks, one at a time. In a bowl,
whip the creams together lightly and fold into
the chocolate mixture. Pour the chocolate
into the loaf tin and refrigerate until set.

To make dark chocolate mousse, melt chocolate with coffee in the top of a double boiler or a bowl set over a pan of simmering water. Sprinkle gelatine over 3 tablespoons water in a small bowl and leave to soften for 2-3 minutes. Stand bowl in a pan of hot water and stir until gelatine has dissolved. Stir into chocolate with butter and beat until butter has melted and everything is well mixed. Leave to cool, then beat in egg yolks. In a bowl, whip cream lightly and fold into chocolate mixture.

Pour dark chocolate mixture over set white chocolate mousse in terrine. Return to refrigerator until set, then cover with overlapping plastic wrap and place in the refrigerator overnight.

When ready to serve, unfold plastic wrap from top of mousse and turn out onto a serving dish. Carefully peel off plastic wrap and serve terrine cut in slices.

Serves 8-10.

Note: Decorate the terrine with whipped cream and grated chocolate, if desired. Either mousse can be served as a dessert on its own and will serve 4 people.

— HOT CHOCOLATE SOUFFLÉ —

2 tablespoons caster sugar
125 g (4 oz) plain (dark) chocolate
2 tablespoons brandy or coffee
4 eggs, separated, plus 2 extra whites
icing sugar, to serve

Preheat oven to 200C (400F/Gas 6). Butter a 1 litre (32 fl oz/4 cup) soufflé dish and dust out with 1 tablespoon caster sugar. Break chocolate into pieces and put into a double boiler or a bowl set over a saucepan of simmering water with the brandy or coffee.

Set over medium heat and stir until smooth. Take care not to overheat the chocolate or it will lose its gloss and become very thick and difficult to combine with other ingredients. Remove from heat and beat in egg yolks with remaining caster sugar. In a bowl, whisk egg whites until stiff but not dry. Fold 1 tablespoon into chocolate mixture, then scrape into egg whites and quickly fold together using a metal spoon.

Pour into prepared soufflé dish, place on a baking sheet and bake in the oven for 15-18 minutes, until risen and just set. Serve immediately, dusted with icing sugar.

Serves 4.

Note: You could serve Dark Chocolate Sauce (see page 117) or Bitter Mocha Sauce (see page 118) with the soufflé.

CHOCOLATE TRIFLE

100 g (3½ oz) plain (dark) chocolate
4 tablespoons rum and water, mixed
4 egg yolks
1 tablespoon caster sugar
750 ml (24 fl oz/3 cups) whipping cream
250 g (8 oz) plain or trifle sponge cakes
185 g (6 oz/½ cup) apricot jam
375 g (12 oz) mixed fruit, such as grapes, ripe pears and
   bananas
grated chocolate, to decorate

Melt chocolate with rum and water in a double boiler or a bowl set over a saucepan of simmering water. Set over medium heat and stir until smooth.

In a large bowl, whisk egg yolks and sugar together until light and fluffy. Put 315 ml (10 fl oz/1¼ cups) cream into a pan and bring almost to boiling point. Whisk into yolk mixture with chocolate. Return mixture to saucepan and whisk over a very low heat until chocolate is incorporated and mixture has thickened slightly. Slice sponges in half. Warm jam slightly in a small saucepan, then brush over the sponges.

Place sponges in a glass serving bowl or individual glass dishes. To prepare fruit, halve and seed grapes, peel, core and finely slice pears and slice bananas. Scatter fruit over sponges. Lightly whip remaining cream, then spoon chocolate sauce over fruit and spread half the cream over it. Continue whisking remaining cream to stiff peaks and use to decorate, then sprinkle with grated chocolate. Chill in the refrigerator until ready to serve.

Serves 6.

NEGRESSE EN CHEMISE

185 g (6 oz) plain (dark) chocolate
5 tablespoons strong black coffee
185 g (6 oz/¾ cup) unsalted butter
185 g (6 oz/¾ cup) caster sugar
5 large eggs, beaten
375 ml (12 fl oz/1½ cups) whipping cream

Preheat oven to 180C (350F/Gas 4). Line a 1
litre (32 fl oz/4 cup) pudding bowl or soufflé
dish with double thickness of foil.

Melt chocolate with coffee in top of a double
boiler or a bowl set over a saucepan of
simmering water. Gradually beat in butter
and sugar and heat until mixture is hot.
Remove from heat and gradually whisk in
eggs. Strain mixture into prepared dish,
cover with foil and place in a roasting tin.
Add boiling water to tin to come halfway up
dish, then bake in the oven for 65 minutes,
until top has a thick crust. Cool, then
refrigerate.

When ready to serve, unmould pudding onto
a serving dish and peel away foil – you need to
do this carefully as the pudding is rich and
sticky. In a bowl, whip cream stiffly, then
cover the cake with two-thirds of it. Use
remainder to pipe cream rosettes round top
edge and base of cake.

Serves 6-8.

Note: The pudding looks very pretty
decorated with tiny sprigs of fresh flowers.

—— RICH CHOCOLATE LOG ——

440 g (14 oz) can condensed milk
90 g (3 oz) plain (dark) chocolate
45 g (1½ oz/9 teaspoons) butter
500 g (1 lb) plain sponge cake
125 g (4 oz/⅔ cup) glacé cherries, halved
45 g (1½ oz/½ cup) walnuts, chopped
45 g (1½ oz/3 tablespoons) stoned dates, chopped

CHOCOLATE FUDGE ICING: 45 g (1½ oz/9 teaspoons)
  butter
60 g (2 oz/¼ cup) caster sugar
90 g (3 oz/½ cup) icing sugar
30 g (1 oz/¼ cup) cocoa

Put milk, chocolate and butter in a saucepan and stir over low heat until chocolate and butter have melted and ingredients are well combined. Remove from heat. Reduce cake to crumbs in a blender or food processor and stir into chocolate mixture. Stir in the cherries, walnuts and dates. Spoon mixture onto a large piece of greaseproof paper and form into a log shape. Roll up in the paper and chill overnight.

Two hours before serving, unwrap roll and place on serving dish. To make the fudge icing, melt the butter in a saucepan with caster sugar and 2 tablespoons water. Bring to boiling point. Sift icing sugar and cocoa into pan and beat well. Cool until fudgy, then spread over roll. Mark lines along roll with a fork to give a log effect.

Serves 8-10.

— CHOCOLATE RING CAKE —

90 g (3 oz) plain (dark) chocolate
60 g (2 oz/¼ cup) unsalted butter
2 tablespoons strong black coffee
185 g (6 oz/¾ cup) caster sugar
1 egg, separated, plus 1 extra white
½ teaspoon bicarbonate of soda
90 ml (3 fl oz/⅓ cup) whipping cream
155 g (5 oz/1¼ cups) plain flour
½ teaspoon baking powder

CHOCOLATE FROSTING: 125 g (4 oz) plain (dark)
    chocolate
155 ml (5 fl oz/⅔ cup) whipping cream
60 g (2 oz/¼ cup) butter
200 g (6½ oz/1 cup) icing sugar
few drops vanilla essence

Preheat oven to 180C (350F/Gas 4). Grease a 1.25 litre (40 fl oz/5 cup) savarin or ring mould and dust out with flour. Break chocolate and melt with butter and coffee in the top of a double boiler or a bowl set over a saucepan of simmering water. Add caster sugar and stir until dissolved.

In a bowl, beat egg yolk with bicarbonate of soda and cream, and stir into chocolate. Sift flour and baking powder into chocolate mixture and fold together.

In a large bowl, whisk egg whites until stiff, but not dry. Add 1 tablespoon to chocolate mixture, then pour chocolate mixture over egg whites and fold together. Pour into prepared tin and bake for 45-50 minutes, until set and spongy to touch. Leave the cake to cool in the tin.

To make the frosting, break the chocolate into pieces and put into a small saucepan. Add all remaining ingredients and stir over very gentle heat until chocolate and butter have melted and all the ingredients are thoroughly combined.

Turn cake out of the tin onto a serving plate. Quickly pour the frosting over cake and serve immediately while still warm.

Serves 10.

Note: For a special occasion, decorate with chocolate leaves and edible flowers. The frosting can be left to go cold, but it is nicest when served warm.

Variation: Omit frosting and serve cake with Dark Chocolate Sauce (see page 117).

CHOCOLATE PEARS

60 g (2 oz) amaretti biscuits
3-4 tablespoons Cointreau
125 g (4 oz) plain (dark) chocolate
3 tablespoons strong black coffee
1 tablespoon orange juice
30 g (1 oz/6 teaspoons) butter
2 eggs, separated
4 ripe pears

Put amaretti biscuits into a bowl, pour over liqueur, then crush biscuits to rough crumbs using end of a rolling pin.

Melt chocolate with coffee and orange juice in the top of a double boiler or a bowl set over a saucepan of simmering water. When smooth, remove from heat and beat in butter and egg yolks. In a separate bowl, whisk egg whites until stiff and fold chocolate mixture into them. Set aside. Peel pears, leaving them whole with stalks intact. Hollow out as much core as possible from the base and fill cavity with crumb mixture.

Stand the pears on a plate, cutting off a small slice if necessary to make them stand upright. Spoon chocolate mixture over pears to coat evenly. Chill for several hours or overnight. Transfer to individual plates using a fish slice when ready to serve.

Serves 4.

— MINTY CHOCOLATE MOUSSE —

185 g (6 oz) plain (dark) chocolate
315 ml (10 fl oz/1¼ cups) double (thick) cream
1 egg
pinch of salt
few drops peppermint essence

TO DECORATE: mint leaves
1 small egg white
caster sugar
grated chocolate

Break chocolate into small pieces and put into a blender or food processor fitted with a metal blade.

Heat cream in a small saucepan until almost boiling. Pour over chocolate and blend for 1 minute. Add egg, salt and peppermint essence and blend for 1 minute more. Pour into individual ramekin dishes or chocolate cups and refrigerate overnight.

To make the decoration, wash and dry mint leaves. Lightly whisk egg white in a shallow bowl and dip in mint leaves to cover. Dip them into caster sugar, shake off any excess and leave to harden on greaseproof paper. Place on each mousse just before serving and sprinkle with grated chocolate.

Serves 4-6.

Note: Peppermint essence has a very strong flavour; use it sparingly.

CHOCOLATE CUPS

155 g (5 oz) white chocolate
juice and grated peel of 1 orange
1 ½ teaspoons powdered gelatine
2 eggs, separated
185 ml (6 fl oz/¾ cup) double (thick) cream
125 ml (4 fl oz/½ cup) thick sour cream

CUPS: 375 g (12 oz) plain (dark) chocolate
45 g (1½ oz/9 teaspoons) butter

To make cups, melt plain (dark) chocolate in the top of a double boiler or a bowl set over pan of simmering water. Stir in butter. Using a pastry bush, dab chocolate over base and sides of 12 cake cases.

Put cases into bun tins to support sides and refrigerate to harden. Meanwhile, melt white chocolate with half the orange juice in top of a double boiler or a bowl set over pan of simmering water. Sprinkle gelatine over remaining orange juice in a small bowl and leave to soften for 2-3 minutes. Stand bowl in saucepan of hot water and stir until gelatine has dissolved. Stir into chocolate with orange peel, then leave to cool.

Beat egg yolks into chocolate mixture. Whip creams together in a bowl. In a separate bowl, whisk egg whites until stiff. Fold cream, then egg whites into mixture and leave until on point of setting. Spoon into chocolate cups and refrigerate until mousse has set. Peel away cases before serving.

Serves 12.

Note: Decorate with blanched julienne strips of orange peel, if desired.

STRAWBERRY BOXES

500 g (1 lb) plain dark chocolate
Whisked Sponge mixture made with 3 eggs, 90 g
  (3 oz/⅓ cup) caster sugar and 90 g (3 oz/¾ cup)
  self-raising flour (see page 104)
3-4 tablespoons strawberry jam, sieved
250 ml (8 fl oz/1 cup) whipping cream
caster sugar, to taste
250 g (8 oz) strawberries or fraise de bois, hulled

Melt the chocolate in the top of a double boiler or a bowl set over a saucepan of simmering water. Stir until smooth. Leave to cool slightly, then spread onto greaseproof paper to a 37.5 cm (15 in) square. Leave to set at room temperature.

Bake cake in a 17.5 cm (7 in) square tin for 20-25 minutes. When cool, cut into sixteen 4 cm (1½ in) squares; trim as necessary. Cut the chocolate into one hundred 4 cm (1½ in) squares (this gives 6 for each cake square and 4 spare in case any break). Warm the jam slightly in a small saucepan, then brush lightly all over sponge squares. Place each one on a chocolate square. Press 4 more chocolate squares round sides.

In a bowl, whip cream to stiff peaks and sweeten with sugar. Slice strawberries if large; leave fraise de bois whole. Carefully spoon cream on top of sponge, then cover with strawberries. Put a chocolate square on top of each box to make a lid. Chill until required, but serve within 1-2 hours.

Serves 8.

─ ICED KIWI FRUIT TERRINE ─

1 quantity Passion Fruit Mousse (see page 43)
6 kiwi fruit
185 ml (6 fl oz/¾ cup) whipping cream

Lightly oil a 1 kg (2 lb) loaf tin. Make up mousse as directed on page 43 and spoon one-third of it into the bottom of the tin. Place in the freezer until set.

Peel kiwi fruit and cut across fruit into thin slices. Arrange 2 of the sliced fruit over top of mousse in rows, then carefully spoon half remaining mousse on top. Freeze again, until set. Repeat process with 2 more sliced kiwi and top with remaining mousse. Return to the freezer until set.

About 2 hours before serving, remove terrine from freezer and turn out onto a serving dish. In a bowl, whip cream stiffly, and use to pipe a 'ruff' down each side of terrine. Decorate with remaining 2 kiwi fruit.

Serves 6.

Note: Select kiwi fruit that give slightly when you squeeze them, but are not too soft.

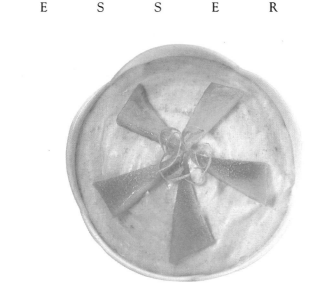

MANGO MOUSSE

440 g (14 oz) can mangoes
juice of ½ lemon
1-2 tablespoons caster sugar
3 teaspoons powdered gelatine
315 ml (10 fl oz/1¼ cups) whipping cream
fresh mango slices and lemon peel strips, to decorate

Drain mangoes well and purée flesh with lemon juice in a blender or food processor. Pour into a bowl and sweeten to taste with caster sugar.

Sprinkle gelatine over 5 tablespoons water in a small bowl and leave to soften for 2-3 minutes. Stand bowl in a saucepan of hot water and stir until gelatine has dissolved. Stir into purée, then put in a cool place until on point of setting. In a bowl, whip cream lightly and fold into mango mixture.

Pour mixture into a glass serving bowl or individual glasses and chill until set. Decorate with fresh mango slices and lemon peel just before serving.

Serves 4.

Note: When folding whipped cream and/or egg whites into gelatine mixtures, it is essential that the base mixture is on the point of setting. If folded in too soon, the mixture will separate out to jelly on the bottom and froth on top.

APPLE CHARLOTTE

750 g (1½ lb) eating apples
grated peel of 1 lemon
90 g (3 oz/½ cup) brown sugar
125 g (4 oz/½ cup) butter
155 g (5 oz/2½ cups) coarse fresh breadcrumbs
apple slices and mint sprigs, to decorate

Peel, core and slice apples. Put into a saucepan with grated lemon peel, 60 g (2 oz/⅓ cup) of the sugar and 30 g (1 oz/6 teaspoons) of the butter. Simmer, covered, over a low heat until soft. Beat until pulpy.

Melt remaining butter in a frying pan and fry breadcrumbs until golden brown, stirring constantly to prevent burning. Stir in remaining sugar and leave to cool.

Spoon half the apple mixture into 4 glasses and cover with half the crumb mixture. Top with remaining apple and crumbs. Chill in the refrigerator for 2 hours before serving. Decorate with apple slices and sprigs of mint.

Serves 4.

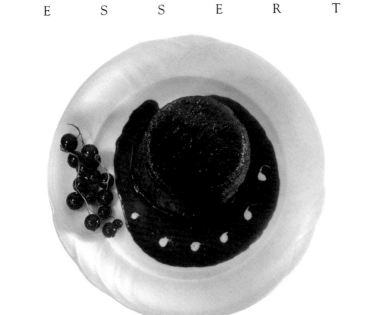

SUMMER PUDDING

500 g (1 lb) redcurrants and blackcurrants, mixed
juice of ½ orange
125 g (4 oz/½ cup) caster sugar
250 g (8 oz) raspberries
12-16 slices thin white bread
extra raspberries, if desired, and whipping cream, to
    serve

Put currants into a saucepan with orange juice and sugar and cook over a low heat, stirring occasionally, until juicy and just tender. Gently stir in raspberries, then set aside to cool.

Cut crusts from bread. From 6 slices, cut circles the same size as the top of small ramekin dishes or dariole moulds. Use remaining bread to line 6 ramekin dishes or dariole moulds, overlapping bread to line dishes completely. Strain fruit, reserving juices, and spoon fruit into bread-lined dishes, pressing down quite firmly. Cover with bread circles. Pour some of the reserved juice into dishes to soak bread. Put a small weight on top of each pudding.

Chill puddings and remaining juice, for several hours or overnight. When ready to serve, turn puddings out onto individual plates and spoon a little of the reserved juices around them. Top with the extra raspberries, if desired. Whip cream lightly and dot a small amount in the juice and serve the remaining cream separately.

Serves 6.

CRUNCHY PEACHES

6 peaches
4 tablespoons maraschino or similar cherry liqueur
315 ml (10 fl oz/1¼ cups) whipping cream
60 g (2 oz/⅓ cup) demerara sugar

Blanch peaches in boiling water for 1 minute.
Drain and peel off skin. Cut flesh into thick
slices. Discard stones.

Place peach slices in a shallow heatproof
dish, filling dish evenly. Pour liqueur over
slices. In a bowl, whip cream stiffly and place
spoonfuls on top of peaches. Gently spread
cream evenly. Cover dish with plastic wrap
and refrigerate for at least 4 hours.

Just before serving, heat grill to very high.
Remove plastic wrap from dish and spoon
sugar evenly over top of cream. Place under
the grill until sugar has dissolved and
caramellized. Serve the peaches immediately.

Serves 6.

Note: Liqueurs are expensive, but there is no
point in skimping for this dish – you need to
add enough liqueur to make sure the flavour
comes through.

— TROPICAL FRUIT COCKTAIL —

juice of 2 oranges
selection of tropical fruits, such as 2 mangoes
2 nectarines, 3 kiwi fruit, 4 passion fruit,
1 pineapple, 1 small ogen melon

MANGO CREAM: 1 large ripe mango
juice of ½ orange
1 tablespoon kirsch, if desired
squeeze of lemon juice
1 tablespoon caster sugar
250 ml (8 fl oz/1 cup) whipping cream

Strain the orange juice into a jug.

To prepare fruit, peel mangoes, discard stone
and slice flesh evenly. Cut nectarines in half,
remove stone and slice flesh evenly. Peel kiwi
fruit and slice crosswise thinly. Cut passion
fruit, but leave flesh in shells. Cut pineapple
in half, discard leaves or use to decorate
serving plate, then peel, core and slice flesh
into chunks. Cut melon in half, discard seeds
and scoop out flesh using a melon baller, or
slice it. Arrange fruit in rows on a large
serving plate.

Sprinkle fruit with the strained orange juice,
cover with plastic wrap and chill until ready
to serve. To make mango cream, peel mango,
discard stone and purée flesh in a blender or
food processor with orange juice, kirsch, if
using, and lemon juice. Fold in sugar. In a
bowl, whip cream stiffly, then fold in the
purée, to make cream streaky, using a knife to
give a marbled effect. Chill until required.
Serve in a glass bowl with fruit platter.

Serves 6.

FLAMING FRUIT SALAD

500 g (1 lb/7½ cups) mixed dried fruit, such as prunes,
    apricots, figs, apples, pears and peaches
2 tablespoons sherry
juice of ½ lemon
2 tablespoons clear honey
½ cinnamon stick
4 tablespoons brandy
90 g (3 oz/¾ cup) toasted almond flakes
60 g (2 oz/½ cup) walnuts, coarsely chopped
chilled single (light) cream or ice cream, to serve

Soak fruit overnight in 625 ml (20 fl oz/2½
cups) water and the sherry.

Put fruit and soaking liquid into a saucepan
with lemon juice, honey and cinnamon stick.
Cover and simmer on a low heat until fruit is
just tender. Discard cinnamon stick, transfer
fruit to serving dish and keep warm.

In a small pan, heat brandy and set alight.
While still flaming, pour it over the fruit.
Scatter with almonds and walnuts and serve
immediately, with cream or ice cream.

Serves 5-6.

Note: The effect of flaming brandy is to burn
off the alcohol and so concentrate the
flavour. It is important to warm brandy first or
it will not set alight.

—————— PEARS IN WINE ——————

2 eating pears
315 ml (10 fl oz/1 ¼ cups) sweet dessert wine, such as
   Beaume de Venise, or red wine
½ orange
½ lemon
60 g (2 oz/¼ cup) caster sugar
cream, to serve

Peal pears with a vegetable peeler, leaving stalks intact. Cut out as much core as possible from 'flower' end, then lay on their sides in a small saucepan: they should fit snugly. Cover with dessert wine.

Peel off as much peel as possible from the orange and lemon halves, using a canelle knife. Alternatively, use a vegetable peeler and peel thinly so as to get no pith, then cut peel into julienne strips. Squeeze juice from orange and lemon halves and add to pan with peel strips and sugar. Cover and poach pears on a low heat until just tender.

Remove with slotted spoon to a bowl. Pour over cooking liquid and leave to cool, then chill for 2 hours. Boil the cooking liquid vigorously until syrupy and reduced by half. Pour the syrup over the pears just before serving. Serve with the cream.

Serves 2.

Note: If you have wine left over from cooking or a meal, pour it over dried fruit and keep in a screw-top jar. The fruit will plump up and gives a lovely flavour to fruit cakes.

——— RICE & FRUIT MOULD ———

100 g (3½ oz/½ cup plus 1 tablespoon) pudding rice
940 ml (30 fl oz/3¾ cups) milk
caster sugar, to taste
grated peel and juice of 1 orange
3 teaspoons powdered gelatine
250 g (8 oz) mixed fresh fruit, such as grapes, bananas
    and strawberries
2 tablespoons whipping cream
2 egg whites
Raspberry Sauce (see page 115), to serve

Wash rice, put in saucepan with milk and simmer for 40-60 minutes, until creamy. Sweeten rice with caster sugar and stir in grated orange peel.

Sprinkle gelatine over orange juice in a small bowl and leave to soften for 2-3 minutes. Stand bowl in saucepan of hot water and stir until gelatine has dissolved. Stir into rice. Leave to cool. To prepare fruit, halve and seed grapes, finely slice bananas and cut strawberries into quarters. Reserve a few pieces for decoration and fold remainder into rice. In a bowl, whip cream lightly.

In a separate bowl, whisk egg whites stiffly. Fold cream, then egg whites into rice mixture. Turn into a glass serving bowl or a lightly oiled ring mould and chill until set. Turn out of mould, if using, decorate with reserved fruit and serve with the sauce.

Serves 4-6.

Note: Turn moulded puddings out onto a wet serving plate. The pudding will then slide easily over the plate, so it can be centred.

PORT JELLY

625 ml (20 fl oz/2 ½ cups) ruby port
peel and juice of ½ orange
peel and juice of 1 lemon
90 g (3 oz/⅓ cup) caster sugar
1 cinnamon stick
5 teaspoons powdered gelatine

FROSTED FRUIT: 1 egg white
small bunches redcurrants and/or seedless grapes
caster sugar

Put port into a saucepan. Using a vegetable peeler, peel the orange half and the lemon thinly and add to port with lemon juice and squeezed lemon shell.

Add sugar and cinnamon stick and heat gently until sugar has dissolved. Leave to infuse for 20 minutes. Sprinkle gelatine on to squeezed orange juice in a small bowl and leave to soften for 2-3 minutes. Stand bowl in a saucepan of hot water and stir until gelatine has dissolved. Stir into port, then strain the mixture through a fine sieve into a wetted 815 ml (26 fl oz/3¼ cup) mould.

Place jelly in refrigerator to set. To make frosted fruit, lightly whisk egg white in shallow dish. Wash and dry fruit, dip into egg white and then into caster sugar to coat thoroughly. Put on a sheet of greaseproof paper to dry. When ready to serve, turn jelly out onto a serving dish and decorate with the frosted fruit.

Serves 4-6.

TART LEMON MOULD

625 ml (20 fl oz/2½ cups) milk
90 g (3 oz/⅓ cup) granulated sugar
3 teaspoons powdered gelatine
3 small egg yolks
grated peel and juice of 1 large lemon
90 g (3 oz/⅓ cup) caster sugar
lemon twists and herb sprigs, to decorate

Put milk, granulated sugar and gelatine into a small saucepan and set over a low heat. Bring almost to boiling point (but do not boil), stirring constantly. Remove from heat.

In a bowl, beat egg yolks together lightly and gradually pour hot milk over them, stirring all the time. Pour into a 940 ml (30 fl oz/3¾ cup) mould. Leave at room temperature until cold, then refrigerate until set.

While mixture is cooling, put grated lemon peel and juice into a small saucepan with caster sugar and stir over a low heat until sugar has dissolved. Leave to cool. When ready to serve, turn out pudding onto a serving plate and pour lemon syrup around it. Decorate with lemon twists and herbs.

Serves 4.

FRUIT DUFF

375 g (12 oz) mixed fresh or frozen fruit,
   blackcurrants, plums or gooseberries, thawed if
   frozen
125 g (4 oz/½ cup) caster sugar
185 g (6 oz/1½ cups) self-raising flour
2 teaspoons baking powder
pinch of salt
15 g (½ oz/3 teaspoons) butter
about 75 ml (2½ fl oz/⅓ cup) milk
Crème à la Vanille (see page 114) or Mousseline Sauce
   (see page 113), to serve

Drain the fruit, if thawed. Grease a 1.25 litre
(40 fl oz/5 cup) pudding bowl and put the
mixed fruit into it.

Add half the sugar to fruit (add a little more if
using tart fruit such as gooseberries). Sift
flour, baking powder and salt into a large bowl
and stir in remaining sugar. Rub in butter
with fingertips until incorporated into dry
ingredients. Add milk and stir to form a soft
dough. Turn out onto a lightly floured
surface, and pat to a circle to fit top of
pudding bowl. Place on top of fruit.

Cover bowl with a piece of foil, pleated in
middle. Tie securely with string round rim of
bowl. Place in saucepan of gently boiling
water to come halfway up sides and steam for
1½ hours. Check water in pan from time to
time and add more boiling water as necessary.
Turn out and serve hot, with Crème à la
Vanille or Mousseline Sauce.

Serves 4.

PINEAPPLE ALASKA

1 large ripe pineapple with leaves
1-2 tablespoons kirsch
1 litre (32 fl oz/4 cups) vanilla ice cream
3 egg whites
185 g (6 oz/¾ cup) caster sugar
1 tablespoon caster sugar for sprinkling

Cut pineapple and leafy 'plume' in half lengthwise. Using a grapefruit knife, cut out flesh. Discard core, then cut flesh into chunks and put into a bowl. Sprinkle with kirsch, cover with plastic wrap and chill overnight with pineapple shells.

Put pineapple chunks back into shells and pack ice cream on top. Put in freezer for about 2 hours, until very firm. Meanwhile, preheat oven to 200C (400F/Gas 6). Just before serving, whisk egg whites in a bowl until stiff. Whisk in half the sugar, whisking for 1 minute more. Fold in remaining sugar.

Pile this meringue over ice cream, making sure it is completely covered. Make small peaks in meringue with a flat-bladed knife. Place pineapple shells on a baking sheet and sprinkle with the 1 tablespoon caster sugar. Bake in the oven for about 8 minutes, until meringue is browned. Serve immediately.

Serves 6.

Variation: Try making this dessert using a fruit sorbet instead of ice cream.

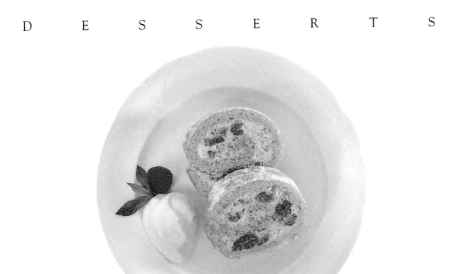

RASPBERRY ROULADE

185 g (6 oz/1 ²/₃ cups) hazelnuts
5 eggs, separated
155 g (5 oz/²/₃ cup) caster sugar
icing sugar
315 ml (10 fl oz/1 ¼ cups) whipping cream
375 g (12 oz) raspberries
125 ml (4 fl oz/½ cup) double (thick) cream

Heat oven to 180C (350F/Gas 4). Line a swiss roll tin with double thickness foil and oil thoroughly. Grind hazelnuts finely in a coffee grinder or food processor.

In a large bowl, whisk egg yolks with sugar until thick and mousse-like. Fold in ground hazelnuts. In a separate bowl, whisk egg whites until stiff but not dry. Fold carefully into nut mixture, then pour into prepared tin and spread evenly. Bake in the oven for 15-20 minutes, until risen and firm to touch. Cover immediately with a damp tea towel and leave overnight. The next day, turn out onto a sheet of foil thickly dusted with icing sugar. Peel off foil.

In a bowl, whip whipping cream to stiff peaks. In a separate bowl, lightly crush half the raspberries, then fold into cream. Spread mixture over roulade. Reserve 6 raspberries, and dot remainder over the cream, then roll up the roulade using the foil to help. Transfer to a serving plate. Whip double (thick) cream thickly and use to pipe 6 large rosettes along the top of the roulade. Top each cream rosette with a raspberry.

Serves 6.

— ICED LOGANBERRY SOUFFLÉ —

500 g (1 lb) loganberries or raspberries
lemon juice, to taste
155 g (5 oz/⅔ cup) caster sugar
3 egg whites
470 ml (15 fl oz/1¾ cups) whipping cream
raspberries and mint sprigs, to decorate

Purée fruit in a blender or food processor, then sieve to remove seeds. Flavour with lemon juice.

Put sugar and 125 ml (4 fl oz/½ cup) water into a small saucepan and place on a low heat. When sugar has dissolved, bring syrup to boil and boil to soft ball stage, 115C (240F). In a large bowl, whisk egg whites until stiff. Gradually pour in sugar syrup, whisking all the time. Continue whisking until meringue is firm and cool. In a bowl, whip cream lightly and fold into meringue mixture with fruit purée.

Divide mixture between 6 ramekin dishes and freeze for 2-3 hours. Transfer to the refrigerator about 30 minutes before serving. Decorate with raspberries and mint.

Serves 6.

Note: For a special occasion, prepare small ramekin dishes by securing pieces of foil around them, to come above top of dish. Keep in place with freezer tape. Pour mixture into dishes to come over the top, so when foil removed, they look like risen soufflés.

LYCHEE SORBET

two 440 g (14 oz) cans lychees in syrup
juice and grated peel of 1 lemon
2 egg whites
mint sprigs, to decorate

Drain lychees, reserving 315 ml (10 fl oz/1¼
cups) syrup. Purée lychees with the syrup and
lemon juice in a blender or food processor.

Stir in lemon peel, tip into a plastic container
and freeze for about 1 hour, until mixture is
slushy and semi-frozen.

In a large bowl, whisk egg whites until stiff.
Tip in semi-frozen lychee purée and fold
together to combine thoroughly. Return to
freezer until firm. Serve the sorbet decorated
with sprigs of mint.

Serves 4-6.

Note: If time permits, whisk sorbet once
more about 1 hour after adding egg whites.
This gives a smoother texture. Serve sorbets
soon after making for the best flavour.

FRUIT FRITTERS

4 cooking or crisp tart eating apples
2-3 tablespoons calvados or cognac
3 tablespoons caster sugar
125 g (4 oz/1 cup) plain flour
pinch of salt
2 eggs, separated
155 ml (5 fl oz/²⁄₃ cup) milk
1 tablespoon oil
oil for deep frying
icing sugar

Peel, core and cut apples into rings.

In a shallow dish, mix calvados or cognac with half the sugar. Add apples, turning them over to coat. Leave to macerate for 30 minutes. Sift flour and salt into a large bowl and mix in remaining sugar. Make a well in centre and drop in egg yolks. Using a wooden spoon, draw flour into yolks while gradually adding milk. Beat to a smooth batter, then leave to stand for 30 minutes. In a separate bowl, whisk egg whites until stiff and fold into batter with 1 tablespoon oil.

Heat oil for deep frying to 195C (385F). Drain fruit and dip each ring into batter to coat. Deep fry a few at a time, turning once, until puffed up and golden brown. Drain the fritters on absorbent kitchen paper and serve hot, sprinkled with a little icing sugar.

Serves 4.

Variations: Use pineapple, pears or bananas in place of apples, soaking them in an appropriate liqueur for 30 minutes.

— CARAMEL FRUIT KEBABS —

selection of fruit, such as 2 bananas, 2 pears, 1 small
  pineapple, 2 peaches, grapes and strawberries
60 g (2 oz/¼ cup) butter, melted
2 tablespoons caster sugar
Mousseline Sauce (see page 113), to serve, if desired

MARINADE: 1 tablespoon lemon juice
3 tablespoons brandy
1-2 tablespoons clear honey
125 ml (4 fl oz/½ cup) orange juice
cinnamon stick, broken into pieces

In a large bowl, mix together all the
ingredients for the marinade.

To prepare fruit, cut bananas into 2.5 cm
(1 in) pieces, peel and core pears and cut in
chunks, cut pineapple into thick slices then
peel and discard core and cut flesh in chunks,
skin peaches and cut flesh in chunks, leave
grapes whole. Add these to the marinade and
stir very gently to coat evenly, then leave for
2 hours. Add whole strawberries to marinade
15 minutes before end of marinating time.

Drain fruit, reserving marinade. Thread fruit
onto 6 kebab sticks, brush with melted butter
and sprinkle with sugar. Place under a
medium grill for 7-8 minutes, turning
frequently. Brush with any leftover butter and
sprinkle with remaining sugar while turning.
Strain marinade into a saucepan and heat
gently. Serve with the kebabs with
Mousseline Sauce, if using.

Serves 6.

SPOTTED DICK

125 g (4 oz/1 cup) self-raising flour
9 teaspoons cornflour
1 teaspoon baking powder
125 g (4 oz/½ cup) caster sugar
125 g (4 oz/½ cup) butter, softened
juice and grated peel of 1 orange
2 eggs
125 g (4 oz/¾ cup) sultanas
60 g (2 oz/⅓ cup) chopped mixed citrus peel
Mousseline Sauce (see page 113) or Blackcurrant
    Sauce (see page 112), to serve

Butter a 940 ml (30 fl oz/3¾ cup) pudding
bowl or a 20 cm (8 in) ring mould. Sift flour,
cornflour and baking powder onto a plate.

In a large bowl, cream sugar, butter and grated
orange peel until light and fluffy. In a separate
bowl, beat eggs with orange juice, then beat
this gradually into butter mixture with 1
tablespoon flour mixture. Fold in remaining
flour with sultanas and citrus peel. The
mixture should be a soft, dropping
consistency (if it is too stiff, add a little milk).

Spoon mixture into prepared bowl or mould
and cover top with a piece of buttered foil,
pleated in middle. Tie securely with string
round rim of bowl or mould and place in
saucepan of gently boiling water to come
halfway up sides. Steam for 1½-2 hours. Turn
out and serve warm with Mousseline Sauce or
Blackcurrant Sauce.

Serves 6.

Note: Wash fruit before using in a pudding or
cake to remove the coating of oil or sugar.

— BAKED DEMELZA APPLES —

60 g (2 oz/⅓ cup) mixed raisins and sultanas
5 tablespoons ginger wine, Madeira or sweet sherry
4 large cooking apples
90 g (3 oz/¾ cup) toasted, flaked almonds
1-2 tablespoons marmalade
chilled whipped cream, to serve

Preheat oven to 180C (350F/Gas 4). Put raisins and sultanas into a small bowl and add ginger wine, Madeira or sherry. Leave to soak for several hours.

Wash and dry apples, but do not peel. Remove core using an apple corer and score a line around each apple. Stand the apples in an ovenproof dish. Drain dried fruit, reserving liquid. Mix fruit with almonds and marmalade in a bowl, then fill the apple cavities with this mixture, pushing it down firmly. Pour strained liquid over apples.

Bake the apples in the oven for 45-60 minutes, until soft. Pile a spoonful of whipped cream on top of each apple and serve immediately.

Serves 4.

KISSEL

750 g (1½ lb) canned or bottled blackcurrants
250 g (8 oz) canned or bottled stoned black cherries
1 tablespoon arrowroot
juice and grated peel of 1 orange
250 g (8 oz) fresh raspberries
2 tablespoons crème de cassis
Meringues (see page 36) or shortbread biscuits, to
   serve, if desired

Drain blackcurrants and cherries, reserving
500 ml (16 fl oz/2 cups) juice. Put the juice
into a saucepan and bring to the boil.

In a small bowl, mix arrowroot with orange
juice and add to juices in pan with orange
peel. Stir over medium heat until juices are
thick and clear; the syrup should boil for 1-2
minutes to cook the arrowroot.

Place blackcurrants, cherries and raspberries
in a glass serving dish. Pour thickened juices
over them and cool. Stir in cassis. Chill in the
refrigerator. Serve with meringues or
shortbread biscuits, if desired.

Serves 6.

Note: Add liqueur to this dish when the
syrup is cold. This way the flavour of the
liqueur remains unaltered.

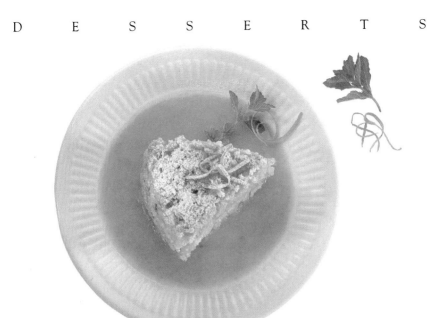

— LEMON BELVOIR PUDDING —

125 g (4 oz/½ cup) butter, softened
125 g (4 oz/½ cup) caster sugar
2 large egg yolks
155 g (5 oz/2½ cups) fresh breadcrumbs
juice and grated peel of 2 lemons
scant 1 teaspoon baking powder
lemon peel strips and icing sugar, to decorate
Hot Lemon Sauce (see page 119), to serve

Butter a 1 litre (32 fl oz/4 cup) charlotte mould thoroughly. In a large bowl, cream butter and sugar until light and fluffy.

Beat in egg yolks and breadcrumbs. When well mixed, stir in lemon juice and grated peel and baking powder. Spoon into prepared mould and cover top with a piece of foil, pleated in the middle. Tie securely with string round mould, then place in a saucepan with enough gently boiling water to come halfway up sides.

Steam for 45-60 minutes. Check water in pan from time to time and add more boiling water as necessary. Turn out pudding and decorate with strips of lemon peel. Dust with icing sugar and serve hot with Hot Lemon Sauce.

Serves 4.

—— TREACLE CREAM FLAN ——

SHORTCRUST PASTRY: 250 g (8 oz/2 cups) plain flour
pinch of salt
125 g (4 oz/½ cup) butter, cut into cubes
1 teaspoon sugar, if desired
2-3 tablespoons chilled water or milk

FILLING: 8 tablespoons golden syrup
45 g (1½ oz/9 teaspoons) butter, cut into cubes
4 tablespoons thick sour cream
grated peel of 1 lemon
2 eggs, beaten

Sift flour and salt into a bowl. Using fingertips, rub butter into flour until mixture resembles breadcrumbs.

Stir in sugar, to make a sweet pastry if desired. Then, using a round-bladed knife, stir in sufficient water or milk to make a firm, but not sticky dough. Knead lightly on a floured surface. Wrap pastry in plastic wrap or foil and put in a cool place for 30 minutes. Resting pastry allows the flour to expand and helps to prevent pastry shrinking during cooking. Preheat oven to 190C (375F/Gas 5).

Unwrap the pastry and roll out on a lightly floured surface so that it is a good 2.5 cm (1 in) bigger all round than a 20 cm (8 in) flan ring or flan tin. Lift pastry on a rolling pin and lower into flan tin. Press gently into sides and trim off any excess with a sharp knife.

To bake blind, fold foil into 2.5 cm (1 in) strips using several thicknesses of foil and press round sides of pastry case. Prick base, then bake in the oven for 15-20 minutes, until dry and lightly coloured. Cool. Lower oven temperature to 180C (350F/Gas 4).

To make filling, warm syrup in a medium saucepan over a low heat. Remove from heat and add butter. Stir until butter has melted. Stir in sour cream and lemon peel. Whisk eggs into mixture, making sure they are thoroughly incorporated. Pour mixture into pastry case.

Bake the flan in the oven for 45-55 minutes, until filling is golden brown and puffed up. Serve warm or cold.

Serves 6.

Note: Serve the flan with whipped double (thick) cream and decorate with lemon slices or strips of peel and fresh herbs, if desired.

PECAN PIE

1 quantity of Shortcrust Pastry (see page 82)
3 eggs
315 g (10 oz/2 cups) soft brown sugar
1 tablespoon clear honey
30 g (1 oz/6 teaspoons) butter, melted
2 tablespoons whipping cream
pinch of salt
185 g (6 oz/1½ cups) pecan nuts, roughly chopped
icing sugar to serve, if desired

Preheat the oven to 190C (375F/Gas 5). Use the pastry to line a 25 cm (10 in) flan tin and bake blind as directed on pages 82 and 83. Leave oven at 190C (375F/Gas 5).

In a large bowl, whisk eggs and brown sugar together until pale and thick. Stir in honey, butter, whipping cream and salt and mix together thoroughly. Fold in pecan nuts.

Pour mixture evenly into baked pastry case and bake in the oven for 20 minutes. Lower oven temperature to 160C (325F/Gas 3) and cook for a further 45-50 minutes, until set. Serve warm, or allow to cool, and serve chilled. Dust with icing sugar, if desired.

Serves 6.

Note: Substitute walnuts for pecans in this pie if you prefer, or if you have difficulty in obtaining pecan nuts.

—— ORANGE MERINGUE PIE ——

1 quantity of Shortcrust Pastry (see page 82)
45 g (1½ oz/12 teaspoons) cornflour
315 ml (10 fl oz/1¼ cups) water
30 g (1 oz/6 teaspoons) butter
juice and grated peel of 2 small oranges
juice and grated peel of 1 small lime
2 eggs, separated
185 g (6 oz/¾ cup) caster sugar

Preheat oven to 190C (375F/Gas 5). Use the pastry to line a 25 cm (10 in) flan tin and bake blind as described on pages 82 and 83. Lower oven to 160C (325F/Gas 3).

In a bowl, mix cornflour to a smooth paste with a little of the water. Stir in remaining water, then pour into a saucepan and add butter. Bring to the boil, stirring constantly. Simmer for 2-3 minutes, still stirring, then remove from heat. Beat in fruit juices and grated peel, egg yolks and one-third of the sugar. Spoon into flan case and cool slightly.

In a large bowl, whisk egg whites until stiff but not dry, add half remaining sugar and whisk again until mixture holds its shape. Fold in rest of sugar, then spoon or pipe meringue on top of flan, to cover filling and pastry. Bake in the oven for 20-30 minutes, until meringue is set and lightly golden. Serve warm or cold.

Serves 6-8.

CLEMENTINE TARTLETS

1 quantity of Shortcrust Pastry (see page 82)
juice of 2 oranges and 1 lemon
470 g (15 oz/2¼ cups) caster sugar
4 clementines
2 eggs, plus 2 extra yolks
125 g (4 oz/½ cup) butter, softened
1 heaped tablespoon ground almonds
2-3 tablespoons Grand Marnier or Cointreau

Preheat the oven to 190C (375F/Gas 5). Use the pastry to line six 12.5 cm (5 in) tartlet tins and bake blind for 10-15 minutes as described on pages 82 and 83. Leave oven temperature at 190 (375F/Gas 5).

Put orange and lemon juice into a saucepan with 280 g (9 oz/1¼ cups) sugar. Set over a medium heat until sugar has dissolved, then boil syrup for 15 minutes. Peel clementines, cut into slices and add to syrup. Simmer gently for 2-3 minutes. Remove clementines to a plate with a slotted spoon and boil syrup until very thick and syrupy. Set aside. In a bowl, beat eggs, extra yolks and remaining sugar together until well mixed. Beat in butter, almonds and liqueur.

Divide mixture between tartlets and bake for about 8 minutes, until set and golden. Set aside to cool. When cold, brush tartlets with a little thick syrup and arrange clementine slices on top (halve the slices for a dainter effect, if preferred). Brush with a little more syrup, then chill until required.

Serves 6.

Variation: Use strawberries or blackberries instead of clementines, but immerse in syrup for a few seconds only.

— CHOCOLATE PROFITEROLES —

CHOUX PASTRY: 60 g (2 oz/¼ cup) butter, cubed
75 g (2½ oz/⅝ cup) plain flour, sifted
2 eggs, beaten

TO SERVE: 315 ml (10 fl oz/1¼ cups) whipping cream
hot Dark Chocolate Sauce (see page 117)

Preheat oven to 200C (400F/Gas 6). Line 2 baking sheets with silicone paper. Put butter and 155 ml (5 fl oz/⅔ cup) water into a saucepan and set over a medium heat. When butter has melted, bring to boil; remove from heat. Add flour and beat until mixture leaves sides of pan.

Beat in eggs gradually until mixture is smooth and shiny (do this in a food processor for speed and ease). Put mixture into a piping bag and pipe walnut-sized blobs onto prepared baking sheets. Bake in the oven for 20-25 minutes, until brown, puffed up and just crisp on the outside. Make a small hole in side of each profiterole; this allows steam to escape and helps keep them crisp.

Cool profiteroles on a wire rack. When ready to serve, whip cream stiffly. Enlarge hole in side of each profiterole and pipe cream into them. Serve profiteroles with the hot sauce poured over them.

Serves 4.

SALAMBOS

1 quantity of Choux Pastry (see page 87)
60 g (2 oz/½ cup) chopped mixed nuts
185 g (6 oz/¾ cup) caster sugar
5-6 sugar lumps
1 orange
315 ml (10 fl oz/1¼ cups) whipping cream

Preheat the oven to 200C (400F/Gas 6).
Cook choux pastry as for Chocolate
Profiteroles (see page 87). Brown the nuts in
an ovenproof dish at the same time, turning
occasionally to brown evenly. Leave to cool.

Put caster sugar into a heavy-based saucepan
and melt over a very low heat. Cook to a
golden brown caramel. Quickly dip each
choux puff into the caramel and then into the
nuts, coating them quite thickly. Replace on
wire rack and leave caramel to harden.

Rub sugar lumps over orange peel to remove
oil. Put into a bowl, squeeze the oranges and
add the juice to the bowl. Crush sugar lumps
with a wooden spoon. In a separate bowl,
whip cream fairly stiffly, then whisk in orange
juice and sugar until cream is thick. Pipe
cream into choux puffs, then arrange them in
a serving bowl and serve within 1 hour.

Serves 4.

BEIGNETS

1 quantity of Choux Pastry (see page 87)
oil for deep frying
caster sugar
Raspberry Sauce (see page 115), Mincemeat Sauce (see page 116) or Hot Lemon Sauce (see page 119)

Make up choux pastry as described on page 87 but set aside after adding eggs. Heat oil for deep frying to 180C (350F).

Drop teaspoonfuls of pastry into the hot fat. As beignets swell, turn up heat under pan so temperature rises to 190C (375F), see **Note**. Cook until puffed up and golden all over. Drain well on crumpled absorbent kitchen paper and keep them warm while cooking the remainder.

Toss warm beignets in caster sugar to coat lightly and serve with chosen sauce.

Serves 4.

Note: Oil should not be at its hottest when beignets first go into it, or they will swell too quickly and the inside will not be cooked.

— AUTUMN FRUIT GOUGÈRE —

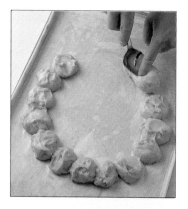

1 quantity of Choux Pastry (see page 87)
500 g (1 lb) cooking apples
30 g (1 oz/6 teaspoons) butter
250 g (8 oz) fresh or frozen blackberries, thawed if
 frozen
30 g (1 oz/6 teaspoons) demerara sugar
315 ml (10 fl oz/1¼ cups) whipping cream
icing sugar, to serve

Preheat oven to 220C (425F/Gas 7). Line a
baking sheet with silicone paper. Spoon
pastry in small blobs onto baking sheet,
arranging them in a 25 cm (10 in) circle.

Bake pastry in the oven for 25-35 minutes,
until puffed up and golden. Split circle in half
horizontally and scoop out and discard any
uncooked paste. Return halves, cut side up,
to baking sheet and bake for a further 5
minutes. Leave to cool. Peel, core and slice
apples. Melt butter in a saucepan and add
apples, blackberries and demerara sugar.
Cover and simmer gently until fruit is soft but
not pulpy. Remove from heat and cool.

Place bottom half of pastry on a serving dish.
Whip cream stiffly and spread in pastry.
Spoon fruit mixture over cream and top with
remaining pastry. Dust with icing sugar and
serve immediately.

Serves 6.

Note: Pastry blobs should just touch each
other – they will then join up during cooking.
Do not smooth out blobs – the finished effect
should be slightly rough.

APRICOT HAZELNUT GALETTE

90 g (3 oz/½ cup) hazelnuts, skinned
90 g (3 oz/⅓ cup) butter, softened
90 g (3 oz/⅓ cup) caster sugar
125 g (4 oz/1 cup) plain flour
250 g (8 oz) fresh apricots, halved and stoned
315 ml (10 fl oz/1¼ cups) whipping cream
icing sugar for dusting

Preheat oven to 180C (350F/Gas 4). Lightly grease 2 baking sheets. Toast hazelnuts under a medium grill to brown evenly. Reserve 8 nuts, then grind remainder finely in a coffee grinder or food processor.

In a bowl, beat butter and two-thirds sugar together until light and fluffy. Fold in ground nuts and flour, then beat to a firm dough. Knead lightly on a lightly floured surface, then wrap in foil and chill for 30 minutes. Unwrap, cut in half and roll each piece out to a 17.5-20 cm (7-8 in) diameter circle. Carefully place on the greased baking sheets and bake in the oven for about 20 minutes, until golden. Cut one circle into 8 wedges and cool all pastry on a wire rack.

Poach apricots gently in 3 tablespoons water and remaining sugar, until just soft. Cool. In a bowl, whip cream stiffly. Transfer pastry circle to a serving plate and spread with half the cream. Remove apricots from pan with a slotted spoon and arrange over cream. Top with pastry sections and dust with icing sugar. Pipe a rosette onto each section with remaining cream and decorate with hazelnuts. Serve within 1 hour.

Serves 8.

CREAM CHEESE STRUDEL

75 g (2½ oz/¾ cup) hazelnuts
250 g (8 oz) cream or curd cheese
2 tablespoons caster sugar
1 egg
grated peel of 1 lemon
5 sheets filo pastry, thawed if frozen
60 g (2 oz/¼ cup) butter, melted
icing sugar for dusting
Blackcurrant Sauce (see page 112), to serve

Preheat oven to 200C (400F/Gas 6). Grease a baking sheet. Toast hazelnuts under medium grill to brown evenly. Set aside to cool, then chop.

In a bowl, beat cheese with sugar, egg and lemon peel until smooth. Beat in hazelnuts. Place a sheet of pastry on greased baking sheet, keeping remainder covered with a damp tea towel. Brush with melted butter and place another sheet on top. Layer all 5 sheets of pastry on top of one another, brushing each one with melted butter.

Spoon cheese mixture in a line down centre of pastry and fold either short end over the filling. Roll up pastry, round filling, and turn it on baking sheet, so join is underneath. Brush top of strudel with remaining butter and bake in the oven for 25-30 minutes, until golden brown and flaky. Dust with icing sugar and serve warm, cut in diagonal slices. Serve the Blackcurrant Sauce separately.

Serves 4-6.

NECTARINE BAKLAVA

10 sheets filo pastry, thawed if frozen
155 g (5 oz/⅔ cup) butter, melted
220 g (7 oz/1¾ cups) chopped mixed nuts
1½ teaspoons ground cinnamon
8 tablespoons caster sugar
juice and grated peel of 2 lemons
1 tablespoon orange flower water
4 nectarines
icing sugar, to decorate

Preheat oven to 180C (350F/Gas 4). Cut pastry sheets in half, and each half into 4.

Working quickly, brush one cut sheet of pastry with melted butter. Line 8 individual 10 cm (4 in) Yorkshire pudding tins with one piece of pastry each. Brush 3 more cut sheets with butter and lay the pieces in the tins, so each tin has 4 pieces overlapping each other at different angles. Mix nuts, cinnamon and half the sugar, and spread half this mixture over pastry. Cover with 2 more layers of pastry, brushed with butter, then top with remaining nut mixture. Cover with rest of pastry, brushed with butter.

Press down pastry in tins and bake in the oven for 20-25 minutes, until golden brown. Meanwhile, dissolve remaining sugar in lemon juice over low heat. Stir in lemon peel and orange flower water. Bring to boil and simmer for 3 minutes. Cool slightly. Slice nectarines into syrup, turning them carefully to coat. Spoon into centre of pastries and dust edges with icing sugar. Serve lukewarm or cold, when pastries have absorbed some of the syrup.

Serves 8.

MINCEMEAT JALOUSIE

410 g (13 oz) puff pastry, thawed if frozen
1 tablespoon milk
1 tablespoon caster sugar

MINCEMEAT: 2 eating apples
2 bananas
juice and grated peel of ½ lemon and 1 orange
60 g (2 oz) grapes
90 g (3 oz/⅔ cup) currants
90 g (3 oz/½ cup) raisins
90 g (3 oz/½ cup) sultanas
30 g (1 oz/¼ cup) almonds, roughly chopped
30 g (1 oz/⅓ cup) walnuts, roughly chopped
30 g (1 oz/⅓ cup) raw cane sugar
2 tablespoons brandy
45 g (1½ oz/9 teaspoons) butter, melted

To make the mincemeat, peel and chop apples and bananas. In a large bowl, quickly toss prepared fruit in lemon juice. Halve and seed grapes and add to fruit with orange juice and lemon and orange peel. Add currants, raisins and sultanas. Add nuts to mixture with sugar and brandy. Mix everything together well, then stir in melted butter. You only need one-third of this quantity for the jalousie, but it is not worth making a smaller amount. Use the remainder for mince pies.

Preheat oven to 220C (425F/Gas 7). Roll out pastry to a 30 x 12.5 cm (12 x 5 in) rectangle. Cut pastry in half, to two 15 x 12.5 cm (6 x 5 in) rectangles.

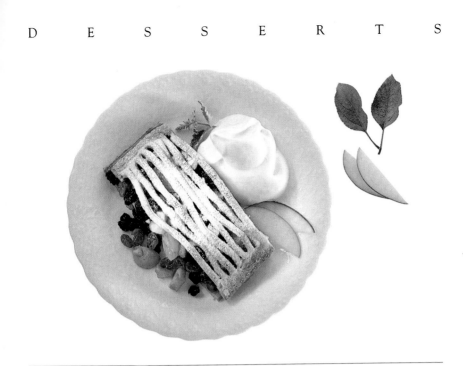

Put one pastry half on a dampened baking sheet and spread mincemeat on top to within 2.5 cm (1 in) of edges. Moisten edges with water. Roll out remaining pastry to 2.5 cm (1 in) larger all round than other piece. Fold in half lengthwise and make cuts down from folded edge, 1 cm (½ in) apart to within 2.5 cm (1 in) of edge. Open and lifting carefully, place over mincemeat and pastry.

Press edges of pastry together and 'knock up' sides using a blunt knife. Chill jalousie for 30 minutes. Brush lightly with milk and sprinkle with caster sugar. Bake in the oven for 30-35 minutes, until pastry is puffed up and golden.

If the pastry starts to brown too quickly, cover it with foil.

Serves 6.

Note: Serve the jalousie with 250 ml (8 fl oz/ 1 cup) whipping cream, whipped with 1 tablespoon brandy and 1 tablespoon caster sugar.

The mincemeat can be made in advance and stored in a rigid plastic container in the refrigerator for up to 5 days.

TARTE FRANÇAISE

410 g (13 oz) puff pastry, thawed if frozen
1 egg yolk, beaten
6 tablespoons apricot jam, sieved
2 tablespoons lemon juice
about 750 g (1½ lb) mixed fresh fruit, such as grapes,
    strawberries and/or raspberries and bananas

Preheat oven to 220C (425F/Gas 7). Roll out pastry to a 30 x 20 cm (12 x 8 in) rectangle. Fold pastry in half, to a 15 x 20 cm (6 x 8 in) rectangle. Cut a rectangle from folded edge, 4 cm (1½ in) in from outside edges.

Unfold middle section and roll out to same size as 'frame' – 30 x 20 cm (12 x 8 in). Place on a baking sheet, dampen edges with water, then unfold 'frame' and place carefully on top of pastry rectangle. Press edges of pastry together, then 'knock up' using a blunt knife. Mark a pattern on frame and brush with beaten egg yolk. Prick centre of case all over.

Leave pastry in a cool place for 10 minutes, then bake for about 20 minutes, until golden brown. Leave to cool. Put jam and lemon juice into a saucepan and heat gently until jam has melted. To prepare fruit, halve and seed grapes, leave strawberries and/or raspberries whole and peel and slice bananas. Brush base of tart lightly with jam and arrange fruit in rows. Brush fruit with jam and serve as soon as possible.

Serves 6.

— STRAWBERRY MILLE FEUILLE —

410 g (13 oz) puff pastry, thawed if frozen
500 g (1 lb) fresh strawberries
315 ml (10 fl oz/1 ¼ cups) whipping cream
1-2 drops vanilla essence
caster sugar, to taste
5 tablespoons redcurrant jelly

Preheat oven to 220C (425F/Gas 7). Roll out the pastry to a thin rectangle and cut it into 3 even sections.

Place sections on baking sheets and prick all over with a fork. Bake in the oven for 15-20 minutes, until golden brown and crisp. Cool on a wire rack. When cold, trim edges with a very sharp knife to make even. Reserve trimmings. Cut half of the strawberries in half – choose even-sized ones for this. Slice remainder. In a bowl, whip cream fairly stiffly and flavour with vanilla essence and sugar. Fold sliced strawberries into cream.

Put a pastry slice onto a serving plate and spread with half the cream mixture. Lay another slice on top and spread with remaining cream mixture. Top with third slice. Put redcurrant jelly and 2 tablespoons water into a small saucepan and heat gently until jelly has dissolved. Brush top slice with a little jelly and arrange halved strawberries on top. Brush with remainder of jelly. Crush reserved pastry trimmings and press into sides of slice with the blade of a knife.

Serves 6-8.

— INDIVIDUAL PEAR PUFFS —

250 g (8 oz) puff pastry, thawed if frozen
2 large, ripe eating pears
1 egg yolk
1 tablespoon milk
caster sugar for sprinkling
Poire William liqueur, if desired

Preheat oven to 220C (425F/Gas 7). Roll out pastry to a rough rectangle, about 0.5 cm (¼ in) thick. Using a pear (halved, if easier) as a guide, cut out a pastry pear shape, 1 cm (½ in) larger than the pear.

Cut directly round pear, leaving a pear-shaped 'frame'. Roll out solid pear shape to same size as frame, dampen edges with water and fit frame on top. Press edges together lightly, then 'knock up' using a blunt knife. Make 3 more pastry pear shapes in same way. Peel and halve pears. Scoop out cores with a teaspoon, then cut across into thin slices. Fit neatly into pastry shapes.

Place pear puffs on baking sheet. Beat egg yolk with milk in a small bowl and brush edges of pastry with this. Bake in the oven for 15-20 minutes, until pears are tender and pastry edges are puffed up and golden. Remove from oven, sprinkle with caster sugar and place under a hot grill for 1 minute. Transfer to serving plates. Heat liqueur, if using, in a small saucepan, set alight and pour, flaming, over puffs. Serve at once.

Serves 4.

VICTORIA SPONGE

125 g (4 oz/½ cup) soft tub margarine or butter,
   softened
125 g (4 oz/½ cup) caster sugar
2 large eggs
125 g (4 oz/1 cup) self-raising flour
milk, if needed

TO SERVE: whipped cream
fresh fruit

Preheat oven to 180C (350F/Gas 4). Grease
two 17.5 cm (7 in) round sandwich tins or a
20 cm (8 in) square tin.

In a bowl, cream margarine or butter and
sugar together until light and fluffy. Beat eggs
in a separate small bowl, then beat into
mixture a little at a time. Sift flour into
mixture and fold in using a metal spoon.
Mixture should be a soft dropping
consistency – add a little milk if necessary.
Spoon into prepared tin(s). Bake in the oven
for about 15 or 25 minutes, depending on tin
size, until top is golden and spongy to touch.
Turn out and cool on a wire rack.

To serve, spread whipped cream on one round
cake and arrange fruit on top. Sandwich with
other cake. Spread a square cake with
whipped cream mixed with some fruit, and
arrange remainder over top.

Serves 6.

Variations: Beat a few drops of vanilla
essence or 1 tablespoon grated orange or
lemon peel into mixture before adding flour.
Ice the cake with water icing, or flavoured
butter icing, if desired.

GÂTEAU GRENOBLE

60 g (2 oz/⅓ cup) hazelnuts, skinned
4 eggs, separated, plus 1 extra white
140 g (4½ oz/½ cup plus 3 teaspoons) caster sugar
90 g (3 oz) plain (dark) chocolate
250 g (8 oz/2½ cups) walnuts, finely chopped
155 ml (5 fl oz/⅔ cup) whipping cream

Preheat oven to 150C (300F/Gas 2). Butter a 1 kg (2 lb) loaf tin very well. Grind hazelnuts in a coffee grinder or food processor. In a large bowl, beat egg yolks together, then gradually beat in all but 3 teaspoons of the sugar, until mixture is light and fluffy.

Melt chocolate in top of a double boiler or bowl set over a saucepan of simmering water, then stir into yolk mixture with hazelnuts and walnuts. In a large bowl, whisk egg whites until stiff, but not dry. Sprinkle in remaining sugar and whisk again until mixture is glossy. Fold 2-3 tablespoons into chocolate mixture.

Carefully fold remaining egg white into mixture – this is quite hard to do as chocolate mixture is very stiff; keep cutting and folding until it is incorporated. Pour into prepared tin and place in a roasting tin. Add boiling water to come halfway up tin, cover and bake in the oven for 1½ hours. Cool. When ready to serve, whip cream stiffly. Turn dessert out onto a serving dish and decorate with piped whipped cream.

Serves 6.

— SPIKY COFFEE BRANDY CAKE —

1 quantity of Victoria Sponge mixture (see page 99)
2 tablespoons brandy
3 teaspoons caster sugar
315 ml (10 fl oz/1¼ cups) hot strong black coffee
315 ml (10 fl oz/1¼ cups) whipping cream
3 teaspoons icing sugar
60 g (2 oz/½ cup) split almonds, toasted

Preheat oven to 180C (350F/Gas 4). Bake cake in a 625 ml (20 fl oz/2½ cup) greased pudding bowl and leave to cool in the bowl.

When cake is cold, stir brandy and caster sugar into hot coffee and pour over cake (still in the bowl). Put a saucer over the bowl and refrigerate overnight.

About 2 hours before serving, run a knife around edges of cake, then turn out onto a serving plate. In a bowl, whip cream with icing sugar until very stiff and spread evenly over cake, covering completely. Refrigerate. Immediately before serving, stick toasted almonds into surface of cream all over cake.

Serves 4-6.

Variation: For a special occasion, pipe rosettes of cream all over the cake, then decorate with almonds and flowers.

— MINCEMEAT CRÊPE GÂTEAU —

1 quantity of Pancakes (see page 40)
375 g (12 oz) mincemeat (see Note)
1 eating apple
1 tablespoon brandy
grated peel of 1 orange
juice of ½ lemon
125 g (4 oz/1 cup) slivered almonds
4 tablespoons apricot jam, sieved

Make and cook pancakes as described on page 40. Preheat oven to 180C (350F/Gas 4). Put mincemeat into a saucepan. Peel, core and chop apple and add to pan.

Heat through, stirring from time to time, until apple is tender. Remove from heat and stir in brandy, orange peel, lemon juice and three-quarters of the almonds. Put a pancake on a greased ovenproof dish and spread with a little mincemeat mixture. Layer up gâteau, alternating pancakes and mincemeat, ending with a pancake.

Warm apricot jam in a small saucepan and pour over gâteau. Sprinkle with remaining almonds and place in oven for 15 minutes. Serve at once, cut in wedges, like a cake.

Serves 6.

Note: The mincemeat recipe on page 94 is not thick enough for this recipe. Use a good quality commercially prepared one.

CHERRY SPONGE FLANS

1 quantity of Victoria Sponge mixture (see page 99)
500 g (1 lb) fresh cherries, stoned
1 tablespoon caster sugar
1 teaspoon arrowroot
1 tablespoon kirsch
315 ml (10 fl oz/1 ¼ cups) whipping cream

Preheat oven to 180C (350F/Gas 4). Grease 8 individual 10 cm (4 in) Yorkshire pudding tins. Divide the sponge mixture between prepared tins and bake for 5-10 minutes, until golden and spongy to touch.

Leave in tins to cool. Put cherries into a saucepan with sugar. Cover pan and cook over low heat until juices run. Mix arrowroot to a smooth paste with 1 tablespoon water and add to cherries. Bring to boil, stirring, then remove from heat and leave to cool. Stir in kirsch.

When ready to serve, place sponges on individual serving plates. Spoon cherries in their thick sauce on top. In a bowl, whip cream stiffly and pipe a border round the cherries. Serve immediately.

Serves 8.

Note: Arrowroot is a thickening agent like cornflour, but it does not turn a sauce cloudy. It is more usually used than cornflour to thicken sweet sauces.

FRUIT CASKET

WHISKED SPONGE: **6 eggs**
185 g (6 oz/³⁄₄ cup) caster sugar
finely grated peel of 1 lemon or small orange
185 g (6 oz/1½ cups) self-raising flour
icing sugar, to serve

FILLING: **315 ml (10 fl oz/1¼ cups) whipping cream**
1 tablespoon kirsch
caster sugar, to taste
250 g (8 oz) raspberries
450 g (1 lb) strawberries

Preheat oven to 180C (350F/Gas 4). Grease a 22.5 cm (9 in) cake tin and dust with caster sugar and then flour.

In a large bowl, whisk the eggs, sugar and lemon or orange peel together until very thick, pale and mousse-like. Setting the bowl over a saucepan of gently simmering water helps with the whisking, but continue to whisk until the mixture is cold.

Sift flour twice onto a plate, then carefully, but thoroughly, fold into egg mixture. Pour into the prepared tin. Bake in the oven for 15-20 minutes, until lightly golden and springy to touch. Cool on a wire rack.

To make the filling, whip the cream in a large bowl until stiff. Flavour it with kirsch and sugar, then fold in half the raspberries. Slice the strawberries and set them aside with the remaining raspberries.

Cut sponge in half horizontally through middle. Put one half on serving dish. Cut a square out of centre of other half to leave a 2.5 cm (1 inch) unbroken frame.

Place this exactly on top of cake half. Fill frame with the cream mixture and top with strawberries and remaining raspberries. Cut remaining piece of sponge in half diagonally and set on top like butterfly wings. Dust with icing sugar and serve within 1 hour.

Serves 8.

Variation: Decorate the cake with cream, toasted flaked almonds and strawberry slices.

— STRAWBERRY SHORTCAKE —

125 g (4 oz/½ cup) butter, softened
60 g (2 oz/¼ cup) caster sugar
155 g (5 oz/1¼ cups) plain flour
30 g (1 oz/3 tablespoons) cornflour
375 g (12 oz) strawberries, hulled, and halved if large
3 tablespoons redcurrant jelly
315 ml (10 fl oz/1¼ cups) whipping cream

Preheat oven to 180C (350F/Gas 4). In a bowl, cream butter and sugar together until light and fluffy. Sift flour and cornflour together into creamy mixture and stir to make a firm dough.

Wrap in foil and chill for 30 minutes. Put dough onto a baking sheet and pat or roll it to a circle, about 1 cm (½ in) thick. Prick all over with a fork and bake in the oven for about 20 minutes, until lightly golden. Leave on baking sheet to cool.

Carefully transfer the shortcake to a serving plate and cover with the strawberries. Melt redcurrant jelly in a small saucepan and brush it over the strawberries. Whip cream stiffly in a bowl and use to pipe a border round edge of shortcake. Serve within 1 hour.

Serves 6-8.

AUSTRIAN CURD CHEESECAKE

60 g (2 oz/¼ cup) butter, softened
140 g (4½ oz/⅔ cup) caster sugar
280 g (9 oz) curd cheese, sieved
2 eggs, separated
60 g (2 oz/½ cup) ground almonds
60 g (2 oz/⅓ cup) fine semolina
juice and grated peel of 1 small lemon
icing sugar
Raspberry Sauce (see page 115) or Hot Lemon Sauce
   (see page 119), to serve

Preheat oven to 190C (375F/Gas 5). Butter a
20 cm (8 in) cake tin and dust out with flour.
In a large bowl, cream butter, sugar and
cheese until soft and fluffy.

Beat egg yolks into mixture, then fold in
almonds, semolina and lemon juice and peel.
In a separate bowl, whisk egg whites stiffly
and carefully fold into the cheese mixture.

Turn mixture into prepared tin and bake in
the oven for about 50 minutes, until golden
brown and springy to touch. Cool for 20
minutes in tin, then turn out and dust with
icing sugar. Serve warm or cold, with
Raspberry or Hot Lemon Sauce.

Serves 6.

Note: For a pretty pattern, place a doily on
the cake, then dust with icing sugar. Remove
doily and serve.

GRIESTORTE

3 eggs, separated
100 g (3½ oz/⅓ cup plus 3 teaspoons) caster sugar
grated peel of 1 orange
juice of ½ lemon
60 g (2 oz/⅓ cup) fine semolina
30 g (1 oz/¼ cup) ground almonds
250 ml (8 fl oz/1 cup) whipping cream
250 g (8 oz) raspberries
icing sugar, to serve

Preheat oven to 180C (350F/Gas 4). In a bowl, beat egg yolks, sugar and orange peel.

When mixture is light and fluffy, beat in lemon juice, semolina and almonds. In a separate bowl, whisk egg whites until stiff; fold into mixture. Pour into a deep 20 cm (8 in) non-stick cake tin and bake in the oven for 35 minutes, until golden brown and firm to the touch. Turn out of tin and cool on a wire rack. Whip cream in a bowl until stiff. Cut cold cake in half horizontally and spread bottom half with half the cream.

Arrange raspberries over cream, reserving a few for decoration. Top with other half of cake. Dust top with icing sugar and use remaining cream to pipe a border of rosettes. Decorate with reserved raspberries.

Serves 6.

Note: Another way to decorate with icing sugar, is to lay strips of greaseproof paper over the cake in a lattice pattern. Dust with icing sugar, then remove strips.

— CHOC CHESTNUT GÂTEAU —

185 g (6 oz/¾ cup) butter, softened
125 g (4 oz/½ cup) caster sugar
185 g (6 oz) plain (dark) chocolate
3 tablespoons strong black coffee
440 g (14 oz) can unsweetened chestnut purée
315 ml (10 fl oz/1¼ cups) whipping cream
marrons glacés, to decorate, if desired

Oil a loose-bottomed or springform 20 cm (8 in) round or 1 kg (2 lb) loaf tin. Cream butter and sugar in a bowl until they are light and fluffy.

Melt chocolate with coffee in top of a double boiler or bowl set over a saucepan of simmering water. Add chestnut purée to butter mixture with melted chocolate and beat until smooth. Spoon mixture into prepared tin and level surface. Cover with foil and freeze for 3 hours.

Turn out onto a serving plate. Whip cream stiffly in a bowl and pipe over top. Decorate with marrons glacés, if using. Let cake stand for 30 minutes at room temperature to soften before serving.

Serves 6-8.

Note: If butter is too hard to cream easily, add 1-2 teaspoons hot milk to it.

WALNUT GÂTEAU

155 g (5 oz/1 cup) stoned dates, chopped
250 ml (8 fl oz/1 cup) boiling water
125 g (4 oz/½ cup) butter, softened
1 egg
220 g (7 oz/1 cup) caster sugar
few drops vanilla essence
185 g (6 oz/1½ cups) plain flour
1 teaspoon each bicarbonate of soda, baking powder
    and salt
60 g (2 oz/½ cup) walnuts, chopped

BUTTERSCOTCH ICING: 2 tablespoons whipping cream
knob of butter
2 tablespoons soft brown sugar

Preheat oven to 180C (350F/Gas 4). Grease
and line a 20 cm (8 in) cake tin or 1 kg (2 lb)
loaf tin. Put dates in a bowl with boiling
water. Leave to cool. In a bowl, cream butter,
egg, sugar and vanilla essence together until
light and fluffy. Sift dry ingredients together
into mixture and fold in with the dates and
soaking liquid. Fold in chopped walnuts and
pour mixture into a prepared tin. Bake in the
oven for 1-1½ hours, until spongy to touch.
Turn out of the tin.

The gâteau can be served warm or cold,
covered with the icing. To make icing, put
cream, butter and brown sugar into a small
saucepan and stir over medium heat. Bring to
boil and pour over cake. Serve at once.

Serves 6-8.

Note: To prevent dates sticking when
chopping them, dip the knife in hot water.

HOT ORANGE CAKE

125 g (4 oz/½ cup) butter, softened
125 g (4 oz/½ cup) caster sugar
2 large eggs, separated
125 g (4 oz/1 cup) self-raising flour
juice and grated peel of 3 small oranges
250 ml (8 fl oz/1 cup) double (thick) cream
icing sugar
fresh orange segments

Preheat oven to 180C (350F/Gas 4). Well grease a deep 20 cm (8 in) non-stick cake tin. In a large bowl, cream butter and sugar until light and fluffy. Beat egg yolks into mixture with 1 tablespoon flour and juice and grated peel of 1 orange.

In a separate bowl, whisk egg whites until stiff, but not dry. Fold into mixture with remaining flour and spoon into the prepared cake tin. Bake in the oven for 20-30 minutes, until golden brown and springy to touch.

While cake is cooking, whip cream stiffly in a bowl with remaining orange juice and peel. Leave cake in tin for 2-3 minutes, then turn out and cut in half horizontally. Working quickly, spread bottom with cream, cover with top half. Dust thickly with icing sugar and arrange orange segments on top. Serve the cake at once.

Serves 6.

Note: The cream will melt into the hot cake, so serve as quickly as possible.

BLACKCURRANT SAUCE

250 g (8 oz) fresh or frozen blackcurrants, thawed if
   frozen
60 g (2 oz/¼ cup) caster sugar
2 tablespoons crème de cassis

Put blackcurrants into a saucepan with the
sugar and 125 ml (4 fl oz/½ cup) water, and
cook them over a medium heat until they are
tender.

Drain fruit, reserving juice. Push fruit
through a sieve with a little juice to make a
purée. Stir in cassis and enough of reserved
juice to give desired consistency. Serve cold.

Serves 4-6.

Note: Serve Blackcurrant Sauce with any of
the following recipes: Vanilla Bavarois (see
page 12), Coeurs à la Crème (see page 22),
Crêpe Ribbons (see page 41), Spotted Dick
(see page 78) or Cream Cheese Strudel (see
page 92).

——— MOUSSELINE SAUCE ———

1 egg, plus 1 extra yolk
45 g (1 ½ oz/8 teaspoons) caster sugar
2 tablespoons cream sherry

Put all ingredients into the top of a double boiler or a bowl set over a saucepan of simmering water.

Using a balloon whisk, whisk ingredients until very thick and foamy. This will take at least 10 minutes. Serve sauce at once.

Serves 4.

Note: Serve Mousseline Sauce with any of the following recipes: Apple Charlotte (see page 62), Pears in Wine (see page 67), Caramel Fruit Kebabs (see page 77) or Spotted Dick (see page 78).

CRÈME À LA VANILLE

315 ml (10 fl oz/1¼ cups) creamy milk
1 vanilla pod
2 large egg yolks
1 tablespoon caster sugar
1 teaspoon cornflour or arrowroot

Put milk and vanilla pod into a saucepan. Bring almost to boiling point, then remove from heat, cover and leave to infuse for 5-10 minutes in the pan.

In a bowl, beat egg yolks, sugar and cornflour or arrowroot together. Pour the hot milk onto the mixture, stirring all the time and discarding the vanilla pod.

Return to rinsed-out pan and heat gently without boiling, stirring all the time, until sauce has thickened sufficiently to coat the back of the spoon. Strain into a jug and serve hot or cold.

Serves 4.

Note: Serve Crème à la Vanille with any of the following recipes: Bread & Butter Pudding (see page 28), Crêpe Ribbons (see page 41) or Spotted Dick (see page 78).

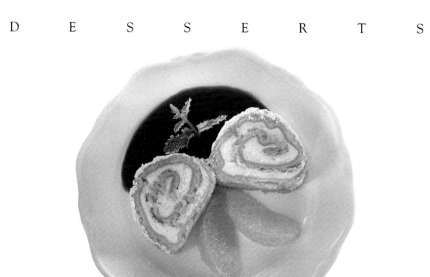

RASPBERRY SAUCE

250 g (8 oz) fresh or frozen raspberries
2 tablespoons lemon juice
60-90 g (2-3 oz/¼-⅓ cup) caster sugar
75 ml (2½ fl oz/⅓ cup) Framboise liqueur or water

Put all ingredients into a saucepan and bring slowly to boiling point.

Simmer for a few minutes, then either serve immediately, or rub through a nylon sieve (if you do not have a nylon one, use a wooden – not metal – spoon to rub fruit through a metal sieve, otherwise fruit will have a metallic taste). Serve the sauce cold.

Serves 4-6.

Note: Serve Raspberry Sauce with any of the following recipes: Cabinet Pudding (see page 18), Orange Roulade (see page 39), Crêpe Ribbons (see page 41), Rice & Fruit Mould (see page 68), Spotted Dick (see page 78) or Beignets (see page 89).

MINCEMEAT SAUCE

2 well-flavoured eating apples
2 small bananas
juice and grated peel of 1 lemon
185 g (6 oz) grapes
22 g (¾ oz/4½ teaspoons) butter
75 g (2¼ oz/⅓ cup) slivered almonds
30 g (1 oz/2 tablespoons) currants
30 g (1 oz/2 tablespoons) sultanas
rum or brandy, to taste

Peel, core and finely dice apples and bananas. Sprinkle with lemon juice.

Halve and seed grapes. Melt butter in a saucepan and fry almonds over medium heat until turning brown. Add prepared fruits with the lemon juice, grated lemon peel and currants and sultanas.

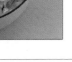

Stir over heat for a few minutes, then flavour with rum or brandy. Serve hot.

Serves 4-6.

Note: If the sauce is too tart, stir in a little brown sugar. Serve Mincemeat Sauce with any of the following recipes: Vanilla Bavarois (see page 12), Crêpe Ribbons (see page 41), Beignets (see page 89) or with scoops of vanilla ice cream.

— DARK CHOCOLATE SAUCE —

185 g (6 oz) plain (dark) chocolate
125 ml (4 fl oz/½ cup) strong black coffee or water
60 g (2 oz/¼ cup) caster sugar

Break chocolate into pieces and put in the top of a double boiler or a bowl set over a saucepan of simmering water. Add the coffee or water and sugar.

Stir over medium heat until the chocolate has melted and the sauce is smooth and creamy. Serve hot or cold.

Serves 4-6.

Note: Serve Dark Chocolate Sauce with any of the following recipes: Vanilla Bavarois (see page 12), Mixed Chocolate Terrine (see page 48), Hot Chocolate Soufflé (see page 50), Chocolate Ring Cake (see page 54), Chocolate Profiteroles (see page 87), or serve it hot with vanilla ice cream.

BITTER MOCHA SAUCE

90 g (3 oz) bitter plain (dark) chocolate
1 tablespoon dark, very strong, coarsely ground
    expresso coffee grounds
315 ml (10 fl oz/1¼ cups) whipping cream
7 g (¼ oz/1½ teaspoons) butter

Break chocolate into small pieces and place in the top of a double boiler or a bowl. Set aside. Put coffee and cream into a saucepan, bring to boil, then remove from heat and leave to infuse for 30 minutes.

Strain creamy coffee through a fine sieve onto the chocolate. Place over a pan of simmering water and stir until chocolate has melted.

Whisk in butter to make sauce glossy and serve at once.

Serves 6-8.

Note: Serve Bitter Mocha Sauce with any of the following recipes: Vanilla Bavarois (see page 12), Coffee Bombe (see page 30) or Mixed Chocolate Terrine (see page 48).

HOT LEMON SAUCE

juice and grated peel of 3 lemons
90 g (3 oz/⅓ cup) butter
90 g (3 oz/⅓ cup) caster sugar
1 rounded teaspoon cornflour

Put lemon juice and peel in a saucepan with butter and sugar. Stir over gentle heat until butter has melted and sugar dissolved.

Mix cornflour to a smooth paste with a little water and stir into the pan. Bring the sauce to the boil, stirring constantly.

Simmer for 1-2 minutes, stirring all the time. Keep warm until ready to serve.

Serves 4-6.

Note: Serve Hot Lemon Sauce with any of the following recipes: Lemon Bavarois (see page 12), Crêpe Ribbons (see page 41), Lemon Belvoir Pudding (see page 81), Beignets (see page 89) or Austrian Curd Cheesecake (see page 107).

INDEX